John Cullender
from FLP. 7/79

For the People:
Fighting for Public Libraries

Other Books by Whitney North Seymour, Jr.

UNITED STATES ATTORNEY

WHY JUSTICE FAILS

THE YOUNG DIE QUIETLY: The Narcotics Problem in America

SMALL URBAN SPACES: The Philosophy, Design, Sociology & Politics of Vest Pocket Parks and Other Small Urban Spaces (Editor)

For the People ✳✳✳✳✳✳✳✳✳✳✳✳✳✳

FIGHTING FOR PUBLIC LIBRARIES

*Whitney North Seymour, Jr.
and Elizabeth N. Layne*

Foreword by James Thomas Flexner

1979

DOUBLEDAY & COMPANY, INC., GARDEN CITY, NEW YORK

✳✳

CONTENTS

"Libraries owe an affirmative obligation to the people. The people have a right to such service, to have someone interpret between the books and those who need them—as much right to know from public servants what books are pertinent to their problems of self-government, as to know from public servants what jellies they should conserve, what seed they should plant, and what hen mash will produce eggs."

Archibald MacLeish
Librarian of Congress, 1939–44

FOREWORD *by James Thomas Flexner*

At the very heart of that American dream which has created all that is most admirable in our society lies education. It is, of course, necessary in a democracy that the voter is fed and clothed, not so that he can become fat and fancy, but so that he will have the opportunity to improve himself, enlarge his knowledge and judgment, and help lead the nation aright.

Does education mean only taking courses? There is today, when institutionalization is conquering American life, a discouraging tendency to regard self-education as obsolete. But surely self-education, once universally recognized as basic to the American spirit, remains basic to all learning. Who should give courses? We hope not a professor who is reading the notes he took from lectures by a previous professor who is reading the notes *he* once took, and so on back to what Eve said to Adam after she bit into the apple from the Tree of Knowledge.

Every time a person—student, professor, or whoever—reaches out for a personal conclusion or a new idea, he is engaged in self-education. Libraries are the capitals of self-education. The young today speak of "doing your own thing." In the arena of knowledge, the most universal and flexible tool for doing your own thing is the library.

Why does the government regard sending citizens to school and often on to college as so important that the opportunity should be furnished free by the state and yet allow libraries to languish? It is hard to believe that this generation has become so mean-spirited that it regards education merely as a means of gaining social status and securing a job. If education is more than that, if it is an expansion of the mind, elementary schools and high schools and community colleges and four-year colleges and graduate schools are tools of major importance; but at the core are libraries.

Public libraries accompany the citizen from childhood to the grave. The preschool child can find on the shelves picture books to excite his curiosity and wonder. If he is lucky enough to have an adult to read to him, books for that purpose abound. And the more underprivileged the home of a boy or girl, the more restricted the budget of the school attended, the more importantly the public library offers otherwise unreachable riches.

As is demonstrated in this volume, the public library must be enabled to call as well as offer, to lure into its rooms those who would not normally find their way there; but for an eager child once arrived and acclimated, what a haven he has found! It is a haven not only because of the volumes on the shelves but because of the aura their very presence spreads, because of the quiet, because of the space, because this is an oasis from all the physical turmoil of the world. Children living in crowded homes, playing on crowded streets can here in dignity and peace seek what they are and believe, seek to find themselves.

Particularly now, when universal education is a national desire, the library has a usefulness that no formal educational institution can rival. "Open admission" has been inaugurated in colleges as a tool to bring learning to all, but it has proved a very unmanageable tool. It demands what is impossible: instruction that will simultaneously serve students whose experience and preparation vary widely. But for public libraries open admission is not a new experiment but the fundamental principle. It is the essence of a library that each individual studies what most suits his interests or needs at his own rate. Guidance is sometimes necessary to show the newcomer where he can best begin to drill his own well of knowledge, but from then on he can at his own pace dig as deep as his time, interest, and ability allow. The most rudimentary information is available and the only limit to the depth achievable in a great library is the ultimate limit of the abilities of mankind as a whole.

The hours adults spend at work are becoming progressively shorter. There was no need to worry about the use of leisure a few generations ago, when men worked from dawn to dusk; when housewives not only had a long progression of children but furthermore ran manufactories of domestic goods in their homes. Now people have more time than they know what to do with. The

Connecticut town I inhabit in the summers contains a covered bridge which used to span the Housatonic in quiet dignity, giving off only an intermittent rumble as some vehicle passed through. Now the bridge is so thronged with sightseers that the town has had to supply, on weekends, two deputy constables—one at each end—to keep order and make passage through the barnlike interior possible. Individuals wander around the bridge long after their interest has waned; they can think of nothing else to occupy their time. How helpful would be a library book, read under one of the trees on the Housatonic shore! Libraries are, of course, not only a source of knowledge, but enhancers of imagination, suppliers of diversion, of pleasure.

Science has greatly extended the span of human life, while our society has been encouraging or forcing individuals to retire at earlier ages. Even when desired, jobs can be scarce. The nation includes an ever-augmenting number of persons who have no essential occupation to fill even part of their days. Public libraries beckon.

Public library doors are open to all free of charge, with no requirement for admission, and irrespective of wealth or race or any worldly condition. When we see people, as various as the community is various, sitting side by side at library tables, each intent on his own dream and desire, we seem to hear the beating of the vast heart—tolerant, compassionate, appreciative, wildly exciting—of a nation dedicated to liberty and conceived on the principle that all men are created free and equal.

But great as this function is, libraries have what is perhaps an even greater function. Libraries are the memory of mankind, the storehouse that contains all which is known and has been thought. Were some holocaust to destroy all intellectual institutions except libraries, all could be re-created. But if the libraries were destroyed, all other institutions in the world could not re-create them.

ACKNOWLEDGMENTS

The research for this book was made possible by the J. M. Kaplan Fund and the Council on Library Resources. We particularly express our thanks to Joan Kaplan Davidson, whose clear vision of the need for broader and more efficient access to library resources has made her one of the pioneers in the citizens' public library movement. We are also grateful to the original members of the ad hoc steering committee which first sparked the creation of a National Citizens Emergency Committee to Save Our Public Libraries: Betty Bernstein, Ervin J. Gaines, Mrs. John D. Gordan, Cynthia Lefferts, Dodi Schultz, Edward E. White, Jr., Michael R. Winston.

We are very much in debt to scores of librarians throughout the country, including members of the staff of the American Library Association, the U.S. Office of Education, and the National Commission on Libraries and Information Science, for their unfailing patience and generous cooperation whenever called upon for assistance. We also express our thanks to Kate McKay for her research into the use of public libraries by American inventors, which enlivens Chapter 4, and to Peggy Reich for her expert coordination of the various stages of the final manuscript. We are grateful for the interest and enthusiasm of our editor, Kate Medina, and her associates, Blair Brown, Ann Hostetler, and Mary Jones, all of whom made invaluable contributions to the final work product.

We express particular thanks to the Trustees of the New York Public Library and to Richard Couper, president, and George Labalme, executive vice president, who assisted in many practical ways to make a national citizens' movement possible. James Thomas Flexner, one of the trustees, has generously contributed a splendid Foreword reflecting the vision he has brought to the work of the New York Public Library. As a token of our appreciation we have all three assigned any royalties from this work to that great institution to assist in making its priceless reference and research collection of man's accumulated knowledge open to one and all.

Whitney North Seymour, Jr.
Elizabeth N. Layne

New York, Autumn 1978

PREFACE

This book is written by and for citizens who are concerned about the future of the public library in America. It is not aimed at the professional librarian or the public library trustee—although both are welcome to make use of its contents—it is, instead, a citizens' action manual for use by people who want to help ensure the future of so crucial an American institution.

This volume seeks to help citizens understand how the public library got to be what it is today; the vital role the public library plays in the life of the nation; and how it can assist in the nation's future growth and prosperity.

This is a "why-to-do-it" book rather than a "how-to-do-it" book, although the final chapter explains where and how the big decisions affecting the future of the nation's public libraries will be made and where an active supporter of public libraries can be most effective.

Although we fully recognize the importance of other types of libraries in the welfare of our country, the focus of this work is on the "public" library. For convenience we set out here our working definition:

> The public library is a community institution, primarily funded by tax revenues, where any person without regard to race, religion, or economic condition should be able to obtain free access to the recorded history, learning, and knowledge of mankind.

Although not sufficiently broad to cover the full range of the public library's role, one apt description is "The People's University."

The public library is the community's principal resource for assisting its citizens in the realization of their inalienable right to life, liberty, and the pursuit of happiness.

The genesis of this book was the announcement on January 12, 1976, that the New York Public Library was being forced to close eight of its community branch libraries because of city budget cuts. The announcement said that eight more branches would be closed the following July 1, and an additional seventeen a year later under then projected cutbacks. One of the branch libraries scheduled to be shut down was the Columbia Branch of the New York Public Library, located on West 114th Street in a racially and economically mixed neighborhood on the Upper West Side of Manhattan. As was the case for the other branches, the library's plan was to break up the collection and redistribute the books.

Residents of the Morningside Heights area served by the Columbia Branch responded to the announcement with clear and positive action. They seized the branch library and staged a twenty-four-hour-a-day sit-in. The sit-in lasted for weeks, and local residents took turns keeping library services going in defiance of City Hall.

The users of the Columbia Branch were not alone. Other branch users also took up arms. They picketed the state capitol in Albany; demanded action from city officials; circulated petitions; organized letter-writing campaigns; staged rallies.

And they got results.

Elected officials were stunned at the widespread citizen outcry generated by the proposed closings. Like so many others, they had taken public libraries for granted and assumed that people would not care whether services were cut back or not. As soon as the politicians realized that they were wrong, they scurried to find money to keep the libraries open. City Hall found federal CETA funds to hire community workers to help man library desks. State legislators increased public library financial aid appropriations by $600,000. The crisis passed, and the branches managed to stay open, although on sharply reduced hours.

Shortly before these events, the manuscript for a book on library history was being completed by Elmer D. Johnson and Michael H. Harris entitled *History of Libraries in the Western World*. In it, the authors asked forlornly:

> Have any people as a majority of a community ever risen up and demanded libraries, public libraries, free libraries, or library service in the same way they have opposed tyranny or taxation, or espoused liberty or a new religion?

After the uprising by community residents on Morningside Heights and elsewhere, the negative response to this question, which appears in the text, could be changed to a most enthusiastic "Yes."

What the New York City experience demonstrated was that there is a tremendous reservoir of stored-up citizen support for public libraries which can be tapped wherever public libraries are threatened. Similar citizen protests have been repeated in many other communities when local budget cuts have jeopardized library services. Citizen support for public libraries represents political power in its purest form. Library users are voters, and millions of library users mean millions of voters. That is the kind of political power which elected officials respect.

Why did the residents of these communities do what they did? Why did they care that much? What difference did the existence of community public libraries mean to them?

The citizen chairman of the local Community Planning Board on Morningside Heights, Richard C. Hsia, explained the reasons forcefully in later testimony before a New York State Assembly Committee:

> There are no high schools within our boundaries; yet there are over six thousand high school-age children living here. The area is home to many families within poverty-level income parameters who can ill afford to acquire their own private libraries. There are over six thousand senior citizens, whose major source of activity and enrichment can be found in a library. And, of course, there are the kids. It is important to remember, and it must not be forgotten, that the branch libraries are one of the few community resources which appeal to, and are utilized by, all ages and all groups.

Mr. Hsia went on to state a vision about the future role of public libraries—a vision shared by many other citizens and citizen leaders throughout the country:

> The branch libraries should be community centers where reality and fantasy merge and interplay, where erudition and job information are equally available to readers.

That is what the fight for public libraries is all about.

For the People:
Fighting for Public Libraries

CHAPTER 1 ************************************

A Short History

When Adolf Hitler's Nazi party came to power in Germany in 1933, one of its first acts was to seize control of all public libraries. Books by Jewish authors were swiftly removed from library shelves. Non-Fascist political writers were banned. On May 10, 1933, giant Nazi bonfires consumed some twenty-five thousand offending books to prevent German citizens from ever reading them again.

Nazi propaganda chiefs recognized the public libraries for what they are in any country—a key to the minds of its citizens. Control of library books meant control of popular thought and ideas.

The realization was not novel. Russia had pursued a similar policy following the Revolution of 1917. Library service was extended widely in the Soviet Union—with bookshelves located in factories and on collective farms, in construction camps, naval vessels, army camps, even on the Trans-Siberian Railway—but all public libraries were (and are) limited to books published in Russia or officially approved for Russian use. Only a few foreign publications were available to libraries in translation, and most of these were scientific. Regular government directives required removal and destruction of obsolete or otherwise undesirable texts.

When the pendulum swung in Germany at the end of World War II, all public libraries in Eastern Germany were placed under the control of the Communist Ministry of Culture, which in turn proceeded to institute a general housecleaning of all pro-Nazi literature from public library collections, replacing it with pro-Communist works.

During the war itself when the Germans had invaded France, they had closed many of its public libraries and purged the contents of others. They also purged a number of French librarians, including Julian Cain, head of the Bibliothèque Nationale, who was sent to a concentration camp.

These episodes are chilling reminders that a key policy of totalitarian governments is control over people's minds through control over the written material they are allowed to read.

The reverse, happily, is equally true. When the Founding Fathers wrote a Free Press guarantee into the Bill of Rights, they were not just thinking of the power of ideas in contemporary periodicals, pamphlets, and books. The writings of John Locke were every bit as important to the thinking of the leaders of the American Revolution as were the newspaper reports of current events in the colonies. It is not simply a coincidence that the American genius of independence, Thomas Jefferson, possessed one of the finest personal libraries in the new nation—so imposing that after the British burned Washington during the War of 1812, Congress purchased Jefferson's library to provide the core for rebuilding the Library of Congress.

When the free public library came into its own in America in the nineteenth century it was, from the start, a *unique* institution. Unique because it was committed to the same principle of free and open trade in ideas as the Constitution itself. Although misguided local officials or library trustees have occasionally engaged in an attempt to exercise censorship over the books placed on library shelves—attempts usually based on "morality" rather than politics —by and large, the public library in our country has been the bastion of liberty. In marked contrast to Germany and Russia, it was a rare public library in the United States in the 1930s and 1940s where a reader could not obtain a copy of both *Das Kapital* and *Mein Kampf*.

America's librarians have prided themselves in resisting efforts to limit the range of material available to library users. This has not been restricted to political ideas, of course, but it is no small fact that the writings of critics of every President and every national administration in our history can undoubtedly be found somewhere in a public-library collection.

When you stop to think about it, the fact comes home that our freedoms and our system of government depend in no small measure on citizens' free access to the recorded history, information, and commentary stored up on the shelves of our public libraries. No government agency or official controls what gets put on those shelves. No government agency or official controls what stays on those shelves. No government agency or official controls what users may remove from those shelves.

THE ORIGINAL NEED FOR LIBRARIES

The very first written records were incised clay tablets and papyrus and parchment rolls. Large numbers of early "books" have been found in ancient ruins in Egypt and the Near East, many grouped in identifiable collections, obvious predecessors of today's libraries.

An insight into the necessity for libraries can be gained from an examination of the nature of these early collections. They were created to preserve vital information that could not be lost.

1. *Government Archives*. Early government records included not only tax and property records, but also laws, reports of military campaigns, communications with foreign powers and military governors, histories of rulers and their reigns.

2. *Religious and Cultural Records*. The priests and their scribes collected and preserved copies of sacred laws, rituals, songs, stories of the creation, and biographies of the gods.

3. *Business Libraries*. In addition to sales, inventory, and employee records, early business libraries also preserved accounts of ocean voyages, trade explorations, natural disasters, military and political events, and formulas and manufacturing processes.

4. *Domestic Information.* Individual families often assembled home libraries of property and inheritance records, inventories of chattels and goods, genealogical and marriage information, correspondence with family members and friends, and sometimes cooking recipes, formulas for household products, and plans for tools. It was in the early family libraries that one could also find the recorded works of a local poet or storyteller, traditional epics, writings on astrology and omens, and works of history or literature.

Taking into account the changes in the nature of man's existence in the intervening centuries, these same needs for preserving recorded data are still reflected in the collections in modern libraries: basic information on government and politics; cultural materials, self-improvement, and books on religion; economics, military, environmental and technical research data; home economics, general history, and literature. The need for access to these types of information has not changed over the thousands of years of recorded history. Details, emphasis, forms may have shifted, but the necessity remains the same.

THE BEGINNINGS OF THE PUBLIC LIBRARY

The first government official to institute a system of state-supported public libraries was Emperor Augustus of Rome. His predecessor, Julius Caesar, is actually credited with the idea, but Caesar was assassinated before he could carry his library plans into effect. Emperor Augustus completed Rome's first public library in the Temple of Apollo on the Palatine Hill in 28 B.C. Augustus' next contribution was an imposing structure built in honor of his sister, Porticus Octaviae, which housed the renowned Octavian Library. Later Roman emperors extended the public-library system throughout Rome and the entire Roman Empire, presumably to spread Roman culture and ideas. In time there were Roman public libraries in operation in Roman-run cities in Italy, Greece, Cyprus, Asia Minor, Africa, France, and Spain.

Interest in libraries came easily in ancient Rome. Earlier cultures had recorded their history on clay tablets, papyrus rolls, and parchment books, and a number of important collections of these had been assembled. The most notable was the library established after 305 B.C. by the Greeks in Alexandria, Egypt, where a copy of every known scroll in existence reportedly was lodged. A close rival was the library at Pergamum, established a hundred years later. After Pergamum fell to the Romans, Mark Antony reportedly removed two hundred thousand scrolls from the library and presented them as a gift to Cleopatra to replace those damaged by Caesar in the burning of Alexandria.

Libraries became prizes of war sought after by Roman military commanders. When Cornelius Sulla led Roman conquerors into Athens in 86 B.C., he seized the library of Apellicon of Teos, which contained part of Aristotle's own library, and carried it off as a war prize to Rome. Cicero reportedly made use of this library in later years.

Rome in time became a city of libraries, with most collections including works written in both Latin and Greek.

When the Roman Empire fell, so did her libraries. Some of the classic Greek and Roman works happily were preserved in the great Byzantine library constructed in Constantinople, ultimately captured in the Crusades. During the Dark and Middle Ages, except for the copying of scriptures in monasteries and the beginnings of universities toward the end of the period, libraries were few and far between. Then came the intellectual explosions of the Renaissance and Reformation and the simultaneous development in Europe of two revolutionary new processes—the manufacture of paper (learned from the Chinese) and the invention of printing from movable type by Gutenberg in Mainz—both contributing to a virtual explosion of books and book collections in the period immediately preceding the colonization of America.

AMERICA'S FIRST LIBRARIES

Books were scarce in early colonial days and most people had precious little time or learning to squander on them.

By the late seventeenth century, however, an Anglican churchman attempted to establish a system of lending libraries through the many church parishes in the colonies. The Reverend Thomas Bray set up seventy libraries in early America between 1695 and 1705; five provincial libraries in the major cities (the most significant being in Annapolis and Charleston); thirty-nine parochial libraries specifically intended for parish use; and thirty-five libraries designed for use by laymen. Upon Bray's death, interest in his library enterprise faded, and the colonists continued to give their attention to the pressing business of clearing the land and establishing and maintaining trade.

More successful were the library collections assembled by individuals and given by them to form the base for America's new colleges. In 1638, the Reverend John Harvard gave his personal collection of 280 books, plus a modest endowment, to a small institution of higher learning founded two years earlier in Newtowne, Massachusetts Colony, which immediately adopted his name to show its gratitude and engineered a change in the town's name in honor of his alma mater. By the late eighteenth century a total of nine colleges had sprung up in colonial America, all of them built around similar library collections.

The most successful early idea for establishing community libraries came from the fertile brain of Benjamin Franklin in Philadelphia. In 1731, Franklin and a group of fifty friends organized the first "subscription library," the Library Company of Philadelphia (which still exists). The principle was a simple one: Each member subscribed a certain sum which was then pooled for the purchase of books to be available to all.

Franklin's model helped to stimulate the growth of other privately funded circulation libraries throughout the colonies. In later

years, Franklin looked back on his role in organizing the Philadelphia library—which he called his first venture into an activity
"of a public nature"—with more than a little pride. Writing in his
Autobiography in 1784, he asserted that:

> These libraries have improved the general conversation of
> Americans, made the common tradesmen and farmers as intelli-
> gent as most gentlemen from other countries, and perhaps have
> contributed in some degree to the stand so generally made
> throughout the colonies in defense of their privileges.

After the American Revolution, the idea of the circulating library spread to the frontier. In 1804, a group of pioneer settlers
organized the Western Library Association, which became known
as "The Coonskin Library" because the cost of subscriptions was
paid in pelts, which were then taken to Boston to exchange for
books.

COMMUNITY LIBRARIES IN THE NEW REPUBLIC

Americans' faith in community libraries as an essential corner-
stone for building their new democracy was put into effect quickly.
Between 1775 and 1800, 20 community libraries were organized
in the young nation; between 1800 and 1825, 179 more; between
1825 and 1850, an additional 551; between 1850 and 1875, another 2,240—a total of almost 3,000 community libraries organized in the first century of the nation's history.

Before long, the idea of supporting community libraries out of
tax revenues rather than relying on private subscription began to
take hold. In 1803, Caleb Bingham established a free library for
young people in the town of Salisbury, Connecticut. By 1810, the
town fathers agreed to contribute tax money to help run the
Bingham Library for Youth. Although intermittent at times, that
public support has continued to this day, with the result that Salisbury's excellent Scoville Memorial Library, incorporating the orig-

inal Bingham collection, continues to provide excellent free library service to the residents of the community 175 years later.

Peterborough, New Hampshire, was the site of another early public library, this one expressly intended to serve citizens of all ages. At a town meeting in 1833, the citizens of the town voted to spend part of its share of state school money to purchase books for a town library, which was housed in the local post office and run by the town's grocer-postmaster-librarian. The Peterborough Library has been in continuous operation ever since.

Public funding of libraries was not highly successful in the early part of the nineteenth century, however, despite various legislative efforts, including Horace Mann's plan for establishing school district libraries, which was adopted in New York, New England, and various Middle Western states. Little attention was paid to the selection of books in these libraries, with the result that many of the collections fell into disuse. But the basic idea of community libraries became increasingly pressing; with growing literacy, legislators recognized that the state had an obligation to provide access to reading matter for those who could not afford private libraries of their own.

Private benefactors also recognized the need, and a number of privately financed "mechanics' institutes" and "mercantile libraries" were established in the country's growing industrial centers to "promote orderly and virtuous habits."

Commercial library operations also flourished, possibly the most enterprising being the "Book Boat" which operated on the Erie Canal after 1830, tying up at various stops between Albany and Buffalo and renting its books for two cents an hour (ten cents a day).

Meanwhile, the new nation was producing more and more books that people wanted to read. James Fenimore Cooper began turning out historical romances based on frontier life. Henry Wadsworth Longfellow's poetry was stirring up sentiment and nostalgia. Ralph Waldo Emerson and Henry David Thoreau were espousing transcendentalism. Francis Parkman and John Charles Frémont were stirring the blood with accounts of the Far West. Harriet Beecher Stowe, John Greenleaf Whittier, and James Russell Lowell were attacking slavery. The writings of Herman Melville and Nathaniel Hawthorne were growing more and more popular. Reprints of English authors like Scott and Dickens were also finding a waiting public.

By the end of the nation's first century the need for community libraries was well established, and a wide range of solutions was being tried, with varying degrees of success. But one problem was becoming particularly clear: Libraries which depended entirely on private financial support faced uncertain futures. The depressions of 1819, 1837, and 1857 all resulted in withdrawal of support for voluntary libraries. A library which cannot keep up with its collections quickly ceases to be of much value. Of the thousands of community libraries which had sprung up by 1875, only 188 were fully tax supported.

THE EMERGENCE OF THE PUBLIC LIBRARY

The centennial of America's birth was marked by an auspicious event, the organizing of the American Library Association in 1876. The beginning of a full-fledged professional organization meant an opportunity for extending uniform standards to all of the nation's libraries. One third of the 103 delegates attending the organization meeting in Philadelphia were from public libraries.

The strong man behind the founding of ALA was Melvil Dewey, who had originated the system of book classification that still bears his name. Dewey later founded the country's first library school at Columbia University (in 1887) to provide basic training in library practices and standards. Writing in the first issue of *Library Journal,* Dewey articulated the dream he shared of an America in which every community had its own public library:

> [I]n an ordinary town we no longer ask "Have you a library?" but "Where is your library?" as we might ask where is your schoolhouse, or your post office, or your church.

Soon a self-effacing little man came along who was to do more to make the public library a reality in America than any other individual.

Andrew Carnegie came from Scotland to America in 1849 as a small boy. His family settled in Allegheny City, Pennsylvania. Two years later, a leading citizen, Colonel James Anderson, opened his private library of four hundred books to the working boys of the town for their use. Carnegie was then working as a bobbin boy in a nearby cotton factory. Every Saturday afternoon he would go to Colonel Anderson's house to borrow a new book.

> It was when revelling in the treasure which he opened to us that I resolved, if ever wealth came to me, that it should be used to establish free libraries, that other poor boys might receive [similar] opportunities.

In 1881, Carnegie was able to keep his resolve by presenting a public library to his native town of Dunfermline in Scotland. A few years later he gave a library to Allegheny City, then an even larger one to neighboring Pittsburgh, where many of his steelworkers lived.

Carnegie then hit upon a form of "challenge grant" which stimulated public-library construction nationwide (as well as in Canada and Great Britain). He offered to pay for the construction of a public-library building for any municipality that would guarantee funds for its operation. By the time he died in 1919, Carnegie's farsighted philanthropy had produced some twenty-five hundred new public libraries. More were built later under the terms of his will.

The independent spirit which permits any American to be cantankerous if he chooses produced some lively resistance to Carnegie's proffered gifts. Some communities turned down Carnegie's money as "tainted." Others debated long and hard before accepting it; the citizens of Detroit, Michigan, debated for almost ten years before accepting a 750,000-dollar challenge grant for a new library.

The result of the various forces at work in the late nineteenth century was to produce an imposing series of public libraries in communities across the nation. By 1913, the U.S. Office of Education counted three thousand public libraries with collections of one thousand volumes or more.

For some Americans the new flood of public libraries came just in the nick of time. The rush of industrial workers from Italy, Austria, and Russia to America's urban centers posed staggering problems of adjustment. Many of the nation's public libraries were converted into staging areas for these newcomers to learn the language and ways of their adopted land. Countless immigrants learned far more than that in those public libraries—they also learned how to get ahead and find success in the promised land. Stories told by onetime immigrants and their offspring about the important part that the public library played in their early days are not only moving, but demonstrate the potential of the public library in developing any individual, whatever his condition or background.

THE AMERICAN PUBLIC LIBRARY TODAY

There are 13,981 community public libraries in America today. They run the range of quality from excellent to poor. Their collections range from broad to narrow. Their sizes range from the New York Public Library with its reference collection of five million volumes and circulation stock of over three million more to the tiny one-room village libraries with only a few hundred volumes that are open to users no more than a couple of hours a week.

America's public-library resources have been developed in a hit-or-miss fashion. By being dependent primarily on local funding and local decision-making, they have been subjected variously to stringent budgets and backwoods thinking; to openhanded funding and gifted leadership; and to every shade in between. Public libraries today run the gamut, symbolically, of short and tall, skinny and fat, backward and brilliant.

The one factor that has resembled a unifying force has been the professional organization which has provided the vehicle for exchanging views and ideas and experiences among the librarians themselves. The ALA, along with other library organizations, has helped develop some very significant facets of American public libraries:

——Adoption of important policy statements, such as ALA's Library Bill of Rights, setting forth the obligation of public librarians to provide balanced and unbiased material to readers on important current issues.

——Establishment of library services for special user groups—children, young adults, students, disadvantaged, blind, elderly, handicapped.

——Providing specialized research collections to serve the needs of local users in fields such as business, the arts, science, education.

——Organizing special programs on different topics to meet user needs or stimulate interest in reading.

——Extending library service through bookmobiles, business branches, storefront libraries.

——Expanding the concept of library collections to include all forms of information and related materials and not simply books.

——Stimulating adult self-education, particularly through readers' advisory services.

After World War II another important force came into play, and that was the concept of public-library systems—combining several libraries to serve larger population units more efficiently. One major cause for this development was the establishment of minimum standards of library service by the ALA. The demonstrable fact that many public libraries failed to meet these minimum standards provided the needed support for state and, eventually, federal legislation to assist in the creation of countywide and regional public-library systems.

In 1956, the federal government for the first time provided direct financial aid to public libraries through the Library Services Act. The object of this legislation was to provide public-library service to rural areas that currently had no such service. In 1964, the law was replaced with the Library Services and Construction Act, which placed emphasis on statewide library cooperation. Five-year extensions of the federal LSCA have been adopted in the intervening years, the most recent in 1977. Since its adoption this legislation has provided a certain amount of funding for library construction, but its most important provision today is the allocation of funds for general library purposes under Title I. Actual appropriations have fallen far short of the sums authorized, and one of the current objectives of the ALA and Urban Libraries Council (an organization of libraries in cities over one hundred thousand in population) is to achieve full funding of the statutory authorizations under this legislation.

Despite these many significant advances in public-library planning and operations in recent years, much remains to be done. Foremost is the need for a stable, reliable financial base to ensure a minimum acceptable standard of public-library service for every American. This means a federal-state partnership.

The companion need is for an affirmative national policy of public-library service to ensure that library resources will be available in a meaningful way to all who need them, rather than simply to those who know how to seek them out.

The tendency of public libraries has been to respond to users who are sufficiently well educated and enterprising enough to use their resources to advantage—what one library historian has called "the intellectual minority in American society"—a relatively small percentage of the total population. What is apparent to anyone who observes our nation and its people is that there are huge blocks of potential library users who may lack special education advantages but who are equally entitled to public-library service and, in many cases, urgently need what the library offers in their personal lives. These are the citizens our public libraries must serve far better than they are served today.

Ironically, one of the most effective spokesmen for public libraries in this century has been the poet Archibald MacLeish, whose appointment as Librarian of Congress in 1939 was opposed by ALA spokesmen and other library leaders because he was not a "professional librarian." MacLeish proved to be an effective advocate for the cause of public libraries and set new sights for the expectations and self-esteem of professional librarians themselves.

Speaking as a prophet for the future, MacLeish asserted a basic principle whose time is now upon us:

> Libraries must be active, and not passive agents of the democratic process.

CHAPTER 2 ✳✳✳✳✳✳✳✳✳✳✳✳✳✳✳✳✳✳✳✳✳✳✳✳✳✳✳✳✳✳✳✳✳✳✳✳

Learning to Love to Read

When municipal budget cuts recently forced a decision to shut down a number of community public libraries in New York City, children wrote letters protesting the action to the library's board of trustees. A very young girl in the Bronx sent the following:

> 3961 Hillman Avenue
> Bronx, New York
> January 20, 1976

Dear Trustee,

   I think that you should keep our liBrary open because Whats' a world without a library. People who are young have to learn to read. If you close the library's those people will grow up dumi and won't know how to read. Library's have bueatiful books. Keep Our Library Open Please.

> Your friend,
> Christine Brummer

   When service in the Brooklyn Public Library was strangled by budget cuts in 1974–75—hours of service down 27 per cent, staff decreased by 18 per cent, bookmobiles eliminated—the children tried to rescue their library with a fund-raising drive. "We made banks and filled them with money so the library could buy some new books."

The kids raised $150 in nickels and dimes.

The reaction of adults to penny collections and hand-lettered pleas too often is tender amusement. We are diverted from the significance of these actions by the charm of spelling errors and the ineffectiveness of the moneys involved (it costs more than fifteen million dollars a year to keep Brooklyn's public libraries in operation). But these children are in earnest and they are trying to communicate something we should take time to consider.

Young people of all ages account for *most* of the circulation of books in *most* of our public libraries—as much as 50 to 70 per cent. Once introduced to the library, they are likely to become eager, avid readers for life. It is the children of this nation, and most particularly the children in urban areas (where 60 per cent of them live), who are the first to be hurt when branches are closed, when hours are cut back, when staff is reduced. Each new child has a whole new world to explore, and nature has supplied a gift of intense curiosity which needs to be satisfied. Remarkable numbers of children read not because they have to, but for the sheer fun of it. A survey of over ten thousand Philadelphia schoolchildren found that 75 per cent of all fourth and sixth graders (nine- and eleven-year-olds) read for "pleasure." But, like the elderly, children are neither as mobile as most adults nor, of course, do they have money to buy the books they want to read.

Legs and bicycles are a child's primary mode of self-propulsion. An adult inconvenienced by branch closings or by short, irregular hours can usually manage to get to another neighborhood where his activities take him, but a child faced with a closed library door or a bookmobile that no longer stops at his corner must either wait for someone to take him to another library, or simply not go at all. In poorer neighborhoods, where both parents hold down jobs, or where car fare cannot be spared from the family budget, the child is often left with no alternative at all. When bookmobile service in the borough of the Bronx in New York City was cut from three vans to one in 1975, the result was a drop of approximately 89,000 in circulation of books in that area. Hundreds of children were simply denied the self-education and escape from the ghetto represented by these contacts with the world of books.

Young people in this country have a greater stake in public-library operations than any other single group of library users. They rarely have a chance to speak up for themselves, and it is therefore a particular responsibility of the adult world to protect and ensure their access to our nation's public-library resources.

CHILDREN AND BOOKS

The founder of the first free library in America was a leading bookseller in Boston, Caleb Bingham, a former schoolteacher. Bingham had an unfulfilled dream of setting up libraries of books just for children, and one day decided to take matters into his own hands. In 1803, he wrote to his brother Daniel and proposed making a gift of a free library for young people from his own stock in his native town of Salisbury, Connecticut:

> I well remember when I was a boy how ardently I longed for the opportunity of reading, but had no access to a library. It is more than probable that there are, at the present time, in my native town, many children who possess the same desire and who are in the like unhappy predicament. This desire, I think I have it in my power in a small degree to gratify, and however whimsical the project may appear to those who have not considered the subject, I can not deny myself the pleasure of making the attempt. I have selected from my shelves 150 volumes for the sole use of the children of Salisbury, from nine to sixteen years of age.

The town fathers were quick to accept the gift, and the Bingham Library for Youth became a reality in the front parlor of the town's minister, Rev. Joseph Crossman. A board of trustees was selected and in due course additional volumes were purchased for the library from town funds.

One of the boys of the town, Orville L. Holley, who later grew up to be a leading citizen, wrote a generation afterward:

> How often and with what delight did I go to Rev. Mr. Crossman's on the Library days to draw my book! Previous Memories come thick upon me!

That same excitement about reading has affected children of every generation from Orville Holley's until today. (The effect on Andrew Carnegie was, as already noted, to stimulate contributions of millions of dollars for public library construction.)

Newspaper columnist Pete Hamill recently protested the announced closing of his old neighborhood public library in Brooklyn:

> When I was a kid . . . the library gave us the world. My brother Tommy and I would get up early on Saturday mornings and wait on the steps to be the first into the building. . . . After a year we exhausted the kids' books and graduated into the adult rooms, and between 11 and 15 I must have examined every book in that building, looking at drawings of life in Ancient Rome, the origins of hurricanes, the history of the English conquest of Ireland, stories of boys who had horses and lived in the West, stories of shipwrecks and mutinies, desert islands and jungle forests. And read Voltaire too, and discovered H. L. Mencken, was chilled by Poe, and died in the Gulf of Mexico with Ambrose Bierce. And all of this was free.

Children can put their enthusiasm in their own words, like this group of eleven-year-olds:

> My mother used to take picture books home from the library to read to me. Now I take my own books. I like books on dinosaurs and I like scarey stories. Sometimes I take home records and posters.

> I got my library card when I was four years old and first learned to print my name.

> In the summer I learned how to make a puppet and we put on a puppet show.

> There are games like checkers in the library that we can play with our friends.

> In the winter I like to go to story hours where the librarian tells us stories and we get to make a wish and blow out the candle.

Libraries give full rein to the many varied interests of youngsters while they are planning their own future lives. An eighth-grade student in Columbus, Wisconsin, recently announced that he was concentrating on his fourth profession:

> When I was young I used to go to the library to get magazines. I used to want to be an airplane pilot and would read airplane magazines from cover to cover. After a while I started to read science fiction books and started thinking I wanted to be a writer. Later I became interested in cars and law. I started reading all kinds of books about both subjects and now I know just how cars and car engines work. So now I can concentrate on law.

A library is more than a storehouse for books. Its availability makes a difference to the quality of a child's life. Nine-year-old Philip Black recently tried to explain that to the director of the Tulsa Public Library when he wrote her a letter protesting the closing of the library branch in his community.

> Do you remember [he asked] when you were nine years old, how much fun it was to ride your bicycle over to your neighborhood library and look through the shelves of books and while trying to decide which one was the most interesting to check out to take home, one of your friends would show up there too? After a lot of deciding on the book you wanted most, you would leave the library with your book and your friend and stop by the neighborhood drug store for a coke and catch up on what your friend has been doing this summer?

There are precious few environments where a youngster is encouraged to pursue his own interests unencumbered by directives from adults. Where else can a child live on a steady diet of literary chocolate bars, so to speak, if that be his or her desire of the moment? A librarian who is skillful will eventually lead the child to try a more varied and nutritious diet. And all the while, as the pages turn, the child is developing a valuable skill. One educator put it quite simply in the *Wilson Library Bulletin:*

> Reading books—really curling up and silently digging through a real book—is the best teaching machine, kit, or workbook invented to teach children to read.

That opinion is supported by research, including an Austrian study on the reading performance of ten-year-olds which established that the number of books read—not the methods of reading instruction, not IQ, not socioeconomic background, as had been expected—but sheer *quantity of books read* was the decisive factor in reading achievement. An examination in this country of two groups of early readers—one in California and one in New York—showed that as a group those children who were readers before they entered first grade held their lead in reading achievement, even after six years of school instruction in reading, over classmates of the same mental age who did not begin to read until first grade. The public library figured prominently as a steady source of reading material for the early readers in the study. One little girl, a black student from a poor family, entered first grade with a reading skill nearly equivalent to the third-grade level despite an IQ of only 91. An examination of her background revealed that her mother read to her often; she had a good supply of children's books at home and she made frequent trips to the library for more books.

Each summer in the United States thousands of children are encouraged to read public-library books through participation in "summer reading clubs," where they earn a certificate or some other award for reading a certain number of books, usually ten or more. The theory behind these programs is that children who participate will maintain or possibly improve their reading levels during the vacation months. An evaluation of a summer-reading program for third graders in Atlanta, Georgia, in the 1960s showed that of the children who participated in the program, 60 per cent gained and 10 per cent maintained their reading levels. Of those children who did not participate in the program, the majority showed losses in reading ability.

Reading is the most important skill a child can learn—not simply making out words, but understanding concepts and unleashing their own imagination and ideas. Numerous studies tell us that adults who are "readers" are more likely to be successful than adults who are not. The usual measurements of success—higher education, higher income, career satisfaction—all correlate with adult reading. Children who read for pleasure are much more likely to become readers when they grow up than those who are never introduced to books. A recent study at the Enoch Pratt Library in Baltimore showed that as many as three fourths of the youngest library users develop a lifelong reading habit.

As research provides deeper insight into the importance of very early childhood development of learning patterns, libraries are directing efforts to reach preschool (three-to-five-year-old) children. Because play is the chief learning activity of this age group, librarians are now supplementing their storytelling techniques with educational toys, games, and puzzles, along with books and other media. Working with very young children, the librarians find that the youngsters have learned to feel completely at home in the library even before they are able to read. From this experience is emerging an important realization about the role of public libraries—the earlier the start the better.

THE EXPANDING ROLE OF THE PUBLIC LIBRARY

Not long ago, the librarian in a small Connecticut town looked up when she heard a young voice ask hesitatingly, "May I use your telephone?"

"Sure," she said to the young girl standing in front of her desk. "Who do you want to call?"

"I don't know," the child replied. "I've run away from home."

With a few questions the librarian learned the girl's name and address and she then went to work on getting the child back with her family.

Children have always run away from home, but today the statistics are alarming. At least one million youngsters, most of them middle class, run away from home each year. Social psychologists believe that ominous statistic to be one result of the dramatically changed status of the family in America. Today more than 30 per cent of America's school-age children live in households where the parents have been divorced at least once. One sixth of all U.S. children under eighteen live in homes with only one parent. A majority of mothers of schoolchildren today hold down jobs outside the home. Six million preschool children have working mothers. For every child who is well supervised, there is another who returns to an empty house after school to await a parent's return from work; the "extended family" in which grandparents and neighbors once took over many child-rearing responsibilities is fast disappearing. Increasingly Americans depend on baby-sitters, schools, nurseries, and, yes, libraries to provide the kinds of support that once flowed from the family and close-knit neighborhoods.

While cultural deprivation is most common among low-income, low social-status families, many children in affluent families, whose physical needs are more than adequately cared for, suffer from the absence of emotional warmth and mental stimulation. Observes Urie Bronfenbrenner, Cornell University social psychologist: "In terms of such characteristics as the proportion of working mothers, numbers of adults in the home, single-parent families, or children born out of wedlock, the middle-class family of today increasingly resembles the low-income family of the early 1960's."

The public library makes a unique contribution in helping to create a desirable environment for the child. Unique because the child enters voluntarily to seek out books and records and games that amuse him (or her), challenge him, help him to understand himself and the world of which he is a part. Here he is recognized as an individual worthy of respect. No matter what his background, his progress (or lack of progress) in school, his interests or hobbies, the child's preferences and desires are responded to. The public library offers an atmosphere that encourages the mind to explore, to stretch out, to extend the perimeters of a child's capacity.

THE CHILDREN'S LIBRARIANS

The highly successful relationship between librarians and children goes back nearly a hundred years. In essence, it is a relationship initiated by the children themselves. They more or less elbowed their way into public libraries, which, with rare exception, had been thought of in the early days as centers of adult learning. Explains Harriet Long in *Rich the Treasure,* a book about public-library service to children, "In some instances [the children] were allowed to come in on Sunday afternoons, or a corridor or alcove was set aside for their use, so that they would not annoy the adults. These corridors and alcoves became rooms as children demanded more space." The 1890s saw the opening of children's rooms in major libraries across the nation. By the time of the great burst of branch-library building at the turn of the century (stimulated by the gifts of Andrew Carnegie), space set aside for children was accepted as a necessity.

Along with the problem of space for children came the problem of book selection. Here the librarians truly pioneered. In the early days of children's services there was no professional group examining children's literature or selecting wholesome and attractive reading from the substantial quantities of questionable "children's books" being published. Public librarians undertook the task of introducing children to the best of literature for their respective age levels. In 1901, a training school was established at the Carnegie Library in Pittsburgh for the express purpose of training children's librarians. As children's librarians became more experienced and knowledgeable about their selection of books, they began to exert pressure on book publishers, insisting on good writing and good design as essential ingredients in books for children. Macmillan responded by establishing the first children's book department in 1919. Other publishers soon followed suit.

Book publishers today depend on public and school libraries for more than 80 per cent of their sales of children's books. Much of the credit for the remarkable growth in children's books—in terms of quality as well as quantity—can be ascribed to the close working relationship between publishers, public librarians, and children.

Observers, including those from other countries, regard the achievement of bringing together children and books as the most distinctive and original service of the public library in America.

The French scholar Paul Hazard marveled in his delightful *Books, Children and Men:*

> Here is an innovation that does honor to the sensibility of a people, and it is an American innovation: the libraries reserved for children. Those light and gay rooms, decorated with flowers and suitable furniture; those rooms where children feel perfectly at ease, free to come and go; to hunt for a book in the catalogue, to find it on the shelves, to carry it to their armchair, and to plunge into the reading of it. They are better than a drawing room or a club. They are a home. And how many children, in these huge cities without tenderness, have none other one but that!

GOING OUT TO WHERE THE CHILDREN ARE

A few years ago, the Queens Borough Public Library in New York developed a mobile "Library-Go-Round" unit to provide a kind of "stepping stone" for kids left out of community preschool programs. Gaily decorated vans traveled the streets of the most economically depressed neighborhoods. At each stop a half-hour story presentation with songs, games, and fingerplays was given. The vans did not simply stop at a likely corner and wait for children to materialize; youngsters were actively sought out. The local poverty agencies helped pick locations and their staff members went into the streets to gather children. Door-to-door canvassing was done. Special flyers printed in English, Spanish, and Italian told what the Library-Go-Round was, and when and where it was scheduled to appear. Library staff scoured laundromats, check-cashing stores, and other neighborhood shops where parents might be with their children.

The Library-Go-Round staff tried to take the same personal interest in the individual child that would be given in the children's room of the library itself. When a child who had always shown up regularly was absent several times in a row at a particular stop, one of the staff would call at the child's home to learn what was wrong and to see if special help was needed. Sometimes they found the parents were not at home and the child had been left alone. Sometimes they found parents "spaced out" on drugs or alcohol. On occasion the Library-Go-Round staff performed such tasks as helping dress children so they would not miss the library van. In bad weather the van drivers and other staff sometimes carried children in their arms who did not have proper footwear.

The Library-Go-Round not only reached its target groups of hard-to-reach disadvantaged children, it also had "a major impact," according to a federally funded evaluation of the project, "on the communications, attitudes, behavior and skills of almost all the children it reached." An overwhelming majority of the parents interviewed by the evaluation team said that their children were more interested in reading, looked through more books, understood better what they read, felt more grown up, wanted to go to school more. One mother of a four-year-old complained, "I can't even watch my TV programs. The minute I sit down, she brings me her library books. I've never read so much in all my life." A majority of parents reported that they themselves were reading more and had learned more about their library. Sixty-eight per cent said they were buying their children more books and were reading the books the children brought home to them.

Unfortunately today there is no more Library-Go-Round for the children in Queens. It went the way of so many programs for children in the tough-money years of 1975–76. Federal funds, which had almost entirely supported the program, were cut off and no local or state dollars could be found to keep the mobile units on the streets.

In rural areas, librarians often have an even tougher time than their city colleagues in reaching the children who are left out of kindergarten, Headstart, and day-care programs. The Northwestern Regional Library System in North Carolina serves a four-county area that has one of the lowest educational and income levels in the United States (only one father in five has as much as a high school education). The isolation built of poverty and ignorance is compounded by geographical isolation imposed by rugged mountainous terrain. Three fourths of the adults have never used a public library and have no knowledge of what services it offers. Many of the county and town commissioners oppose public-library appropriations because they consider libraries to be nothing but a "Luxury for the Leisure Class." Almost all of the preschool children in the four-county area, roughly 90 per cent, are not reached by any preschool program at all.

To help combat the disadvantage these children face when starting school, the library system devised a federally funded demonstration program aimed directly at three-to-five-year-old children. The librarians found that many of the neediest children in the region were never listed with any social-service agency. In the poorest areas, door-to-door searches were conducted; bookmobile librarians were asked to inquire along their routes; mental health departments, doctors, dentists, and church groups were asked to help spread the word; a campaign of public education about the needs of early childhood training in the home was implemented. One by one the whereabouts of the children were located and the follow-up program got under way.

Specially trained library staff went into homes to instruct parents and baby-sitters in the use of educational toys, books, and games that were made available to them by the library. The library published a booklet, "Play Is Work, Too," filled with simple suggestions for things parents and baby-sitters can do with preschoolers to help them learn about shapes and colors and numbers. To provide group experience, a library van periodically transported the youngsters to the nearest public library for a story hour and a chance to select and check out books. For children who lived too far away from the library for group participation, bookmobile service filled the gap. "For most of these children," says Barbara East, coordinator of the program, "it was the first visit to the library, and for many, the first contact anyone in the family had experienced."

In neighboring Rockingham County in North Carolina a bookmobile equipped with shelves for paperbacks, rods for toys and puzzles, tapes and records travels about eight hundred miles a month, to reach economically and socially deprived children from ages three to twelve, and their parents and older brothers and sisters as well. Trish Gwyn, the professional librarian who travels with the bookmobile, reports that children, parents, teachers, and agency directors wait in eager anticipation for each visit and that "youngsters who never had a book in their home before are checking out paperbacks for themselves and members of their families." Branch libraries in the areas served by the bookmobile report that the service has fostered much more interest in library usage by children of all ages.

In cities and rural areas across the land the need for making greater use of public-library children's services in a new and creative way is more and more apparent.

SERVING THE FAMILY

In an effort to strengthen the role of the family as the most fundamental influence on a child's development, much library work with preschoolers involves work with the parents as well. The Cambria County (Pennsylvania) Library System has set aside part of its library as a multimedia environment for preschoolers and their parents, a place for parents to work with their own children and to observe them in a learning situation. Toys for the Preschool Adventure Library are selected to stimulate imagination, socialization, cognitive development, or physical coordination. A toy with large, thick pieces will encourage gross motor development in a young child. A building material with fine, interlocking pieces will develop eye and hand coordination in a somewhat older child. Linda Shannon, who set up the program, wrote about it in *Library Journal:*

> Parents seem to enjoy coming to the Preschool Adventure Library as much as the children. In a community which is primarily rural and suburban, children play either outside or in their basements, so parents don't have the opportunity to observe their children in either play or learning situations.

PAL provides a place where mothers can go with their preschoolers and infants simply to get out of the house. They are able to observe preschoolers other than their own and to communicate with other mothers. Evening workshops teach parents how to make puppets, terraria, stuffed dinosaurs, and other inexpensive toys. Books on child development, crafts, and children's games are readily available.

A number of children's rooms in larger libraries maintain shelves for parents with material on child care. One children's librarian gathered up books about child development from the adult department and placed them in a bin in the children's library. She couldn't keep up with the demand.

Children's librarians are constantly looking for new ways to involve parents. One center-city library distributes flyers in nearby office buildings, offering a special service to parents who wish to telephone in book requests for their children so they will be ready for pickup during the lunch hour.

Weekends, however, are the favorite time for families to use libraries, and those that offer Sunday-afternoon hours report that more than half of the circulation in the children's library occurs on weekends.

LIBRARY SERVICES FOR HANDICAPPED CHILDREN

Beginning in 1975, the Akron-Summit County Public Library in Ohio has reached deaf school-age children and their families through Saturday-afternoon story hours, given in sign language by well-known members of the local deaf community. Jane Biehl, a hearing-impaired librarian, worked with the local deaf community to establish the program.

Hundreds of libraries, including at least twenty-six of the public libraries in Nassau County (New York), make available picture books in signed English for young readers with hearing difficulties. Titles include *Little Red Riding Hood* and *Goldilocks and the Three Bears*. The books are prepared under the supervision of the staff of the Preschool Signed English Project at Gallaudet College, the only liberal arts college in the world for the deaf. Signed English uses both sign words, to represent English words, and sign markers, which indicate possessive, singular or plural, and past, present, or future tense. Gallaudet College has also developed *A Basic Preschool Signed English Dictionary* and an alphabet book, called *Handtalk*. In addition to helping hearing-impaired children develop language skills, these books provide a bridge for communication between deaf and hearing children. A special collection of picture books with text in both Braille and in regular print is available to the general public in the children's room at the Cincinnati and Hamilton County (Ohio) main library. The books are not only for blind children who come to the library but also for blind parents who want to read to their sighted children, for older children to read to younger brothers and sisters, or simply for children who are curious about the kind of books blind children read. Under the direction of Coy Kate Hunsucker, a specialist in work with exceptional children, the Cincinnati and Hamilton County Public Library has active programs for blind and physically handicapped children. She feels that summer library programs, important for all children, are particularly helpful for these exceptional children who cannot so easily find their own amusement. They are encouraged to participate with their peers in the regular summer reading club sponsored by the children's department. The blind and handicapped children are invited to the library for a summer party—a singalong with a young guitarist, stories, or a puppet show, a tour of the library to meet the staff, and, of course, refreshments. At the same time the children are invited to the library party, they are sent information about the summer reading club. The children are encouraged to go to or telephone their nearest branch library for information. Children's librarians are alerted to the fact that handicapped children may be coming to their branches, and wherever possible, names are given to the librarians so that they can make a special effort to include them. "Although most of the children are unable to get to the library in person," says Ms. Hunsucker, "they know they are welcome." And indeed, many of them learn to phone the librarians. Certificates are given to youngsters who read at least ten books; however, allowances are made for those who have severe handicaps which make reading very difficult. Certificates are mailed or delivered in person to children who can't get to the library.

Children who are blind or physically handicapped in such a

way that they cannot read conventional print also have access to reading materials—talking books, cassette tapes, and Braille—from their nearest regional library for the blind and physically handicapped.

Cincinnati also works with hospitalized children. They maintain permanent deposit collections in three regular hospitals. In addition, staff from the Exceptional Children's Division regularly tell stories and introduce books to the classes provided for the children in each of the hospitals. Humor is usually a successful theme for these small groups of youngsters who may not be feeling well. *The Cat in the Hat* and *Curious George* are in constant demand. Librarians also go from bed to bed in the wards—a few words about a funny character in a story may catch an indifferent child's interest and cause him to take a book to read. Sometimes the librarian will stop by a bed long enough to read a complete story.

On a monthly basis, Cincinnati librarians visit classes in a school for preschool and trainable retarded cerebral palsied children. Here the challenge is to pick stories with a simple but active plot involving situations with which the children can identify. Book illustrations must be realistic enough to be easily recognizable, with few enough objects on each page so that the children can distinguish one from another. Because their attention spans are short, they need to be brought into the story by asking them to imitate animals, locate objects on a page, or guess what is about to happen.

When working with cerebral palsied children who are nonverbal, the librarian must remember to ask questions that can be answered by gestures for "yes" and "no." These children also enjoy puppets, tactile objects, and flannel-board stories.

In Gloucester City, New Jersey, public-library storytellers visit handicapped children in their homes. In the one-to-one storytelling, the same storyteller visits the same child over a period of time. Some thirty children are currently benefiting from the program.

The parents of handicapped children also have exceptional needs for specialized advice, information, and materials. Marguerite Dodson at Brooklyn Public Library has put together a kit which includes such carefully selected items as a directory of agencies, factual information on handicaps, annotated bibliographies, and material on child abuse and children's rights. Two kits are available in each branch—one for permanent reference, one for circulation. The packet is updated regularly.

Medford (Massachusetts) Public Library in cooperation with the Medford School Department has organized a resource room for parents of handicapped children, housing a select collection of books, instructional materials, and audio-visual aids that offer a wide range of services and opportunities for parents to help their handicapped children. Parents may borrow the materials and may also consult with two special education teachers at the center who are there to advise them on materials and teaching methods helpful in meeting their child's specific needs for both day-to-day care and overall development. Parent/teacher meetings, lecture programs, films, and demonstrations of instructional materials are held. Parent groups have been formed to allow for idea exchanges and a sharing of experiences among parents of children with special needs.

A CHILDREN'S STORY FOR GROWN-UPS

Once upon a time, not very long ago, two dedicated librarians pushed a baby carriage full of paperback books through the hot summer streets of East Providence, Rhode Island. Louise Dolan and her co-worker stopped their baby buggy at the corner of Leonard and North Country streets, where a group of children was waiting for them in the semishade of the porch of one of the houses. Across the street behind a heavy chain fence there was a little boy, screaming at the top of his lungs. His mother was in the process of locking him in the fenced yard.

Louise Dolan crossed over to the mother and explained that she was from the public library. She told her that she and her friend came to this neighborhood every week during the summer to tell stories and lend books to the children. She asked the mother to let the boy join the group. "No," his mother said, "Eddie is too bad.

He is wild." The librarian pressed Eddie's mother to change her mind. "He was the most beautiful child I had ever seen," Ms. Dolan recalled recently. "He looked intelligent, alert, and alive. I didn't care if he ripped up everything. I believed I had power on my side—the power of books and stories—and I wanted Eddie to have the chance to choose."

Finally, the mother gave in.

His mother had been right—Eddie *was* wild. He ran in circles on the grass. He jumped and shouted. He kept at a distrustful distance. But he did take a book—Maud and Miska Petersham's *The Box with Red Wheels*.

Eddie kept the book throughout the eight weeks of the Street Storytime program. He never joined the group. He continued to run in circles, to jump and shout. His mother was embarrassed but she continued to let him cross the street. Eddie held on to *The Box with Red Wheels*. It became worn; the edges frayed and curled. Finally, the end of the summer came and all books were to be returned in exchange for balloons. Eddie became frantic. He wanted to keep his book. Louise Dolan said, sure, he could keep it.

The librarians returned to the same corner the following summer. There was Eddie, waiting for them, *The Box with Red Wheels*, a tightly rolled spiral in his hand. He eventually joined the group that summer. "He loved stories," recalled Louise Dolan. "He loved the fingerplays and songs. And he loved the games we sometimes played." He still held on to *The Box with Red Wheels*.

One morning that summer, Eddie put the book into the buggy at the beginning of a session just the same as the other children did. After the stories, Louise Dolan said, "Let's find a book for this week." Eddie worked his way into the cluster around the buggy and snatched up Richard Scarry's *Cars and Trucks and Things That Go*. He kept this book, prized and dearly loved, for the remainder of the summer.

The next time the librarian saw Eddie was one afternoon the following winter, when she was waiting at the public library to begin her story hour for the children from Saint Benedict's Hearth, a nearby day-care center. There was Eddie among the four- and five-year-olds seating themselves on the library's blue rug. He sat there attentively, waiting for the story hour to begin—just like the other children.

"Eddie was extraordinary," observes Ms. Dolan. "But what happened was ordinary: A child had the opportunity to hear stories, to be read to, to share a book, to have books for himself, and he had liked the experience and wanted more."

CHAPTER 3 ✶✶✶✶✶✶✶✶✶✶✶✶✶✶✶✶✶✶✶✶✶✶✶✶✶✶✶✶✶✶✶✶✶✶✶✶✶

Students Young and Old

When Jacob K. Javits was elected to the United States Senate in 1957, the event reminded many people that America was still a land of tremendous opportunity. Javits had literally come up from the streets, against the odds, using his native intelligence and the community's free resources—the public school and the public library. Javits, New York's senior senator and a foreign- and urban-policy leader, speaks feelingly about his humble beginnings:

> I was born in 1904, and I remember vividly my life as a small boy, the son of Jewish immigrants, in a janitor's flat on Orchard and Stanton streets on the Lower East Side of New York City. My father made pants and doubled as janitor of the tenement, then later worked full time as the janitor for $30 a month, plus rooms. My mother sold crockery and dry goods from a pushcart. In school I read about democracy and about the equality of all in America, but to a poor Jewish boy, running errands for a candy shop, scratching for a penny, watching my father get out the vote for two dollars a head paid by a saloonkeeper who was a Tammany Hall captain, the words "democracy" and "equality" seemed just so many distant, high-sounding phrases.

The future senator's parents had both faced great odds when they came to this country. His father, Morris Javits, was born in what is now the Soviet Ukraine, and came here virtually penniless at the age of twenty-two. The only work he could find was seasonal employment in the clothing industry. In the United States he met and married Ida Littman, herself an immigrant from Odessa at eighteen. She could neither read nor write but managed somehow to earn a living making neckties. There were two Javits sons, who grew up among old-law tenements and attended the neighborhood public school, which had its limitations. The place where the future United States senator found the educational experience he yearned for was at the Rivington Street Public Library.

During Senate hearings on extension of the Library Services and Construction Act in 1977, Javits looked back on his days at the public library and the important part it had played in his education.

> I am sure I would not be here were it not for the Rivington Street Public Library and the amount of extra schoolwork I was able to do. And I know other kids just like me who had exactly the same experience, who have had an appetite for learning, and you couldn't possibly satisfy it on a regular curriculum.

Although his achievements have been unusual, Javits' use of the public library was not. For many young Americans from all kinds of backgrounds, the free public library is the first rung on the ladder of success. Second only to the classroom, it continues to be the most important educational resource in any community in the nation.

PUBLIC LIBRARIES AND FORMAL EDUCATION

The affinity between formal education and the public library is a long-standing one. In 1876, in a *Special Report on Public Libraries in the United States,* the U.S. Bureau of Education called public libraries "auxiliaries" to public education, and said that librarians should come to understand their special responsibilities as "teachers." Over the years, public libraries have added special staffs, acquired additional volumes, and organized new departments to enable them to serve schools more adequately.

Formal education is one of the areas that has benefited most directly from the free public-library system. In the decades since World War II, the nation's burgeoning and more sophisticated student population has become the largest single category of users of public libraries. In spite of the rapid growth in school and college libraries—a growth stimulated in large part by massive infusions of federal dollars—student demands on public libraries are today greater than ever. These demands are not simply the result of sheer numbers. They are also the result of the "graying" of the student population, as more older people return to the classroom. (The median age in community colleges has already reached twenty-eight.) The demands placed on reference librarians yearly grow more complex and challenging, in turn forcing librarians themselves back to the classroom so they can keep pace.

Student use of public libraries to supplement the libraries of their own academic institutions is a well-established matter of record. When public libraries, like the schools and colleges, were reeling from the impact of the postwar baby boom in the 1960s, a number of them took a look at just who their users were. An examination of the library habits of students in eighty institutions of higher education in New York City revealed that more than eight out of ten students used some other library in addition to the one in their respective schools, and that half of them did so at least once a month. (Monthly use of a library is generally considered to be "heavy" use.) Public libraries, it was found, provided the greatest part of this additional service. The authors of the study concluded that "most of New York's higher education students use, and use heavily, the wealth of library resources available to them in New York City to supplement, and, no doubt, in some instances to supplant the libraries provided at their own schools." Every third student considered the book collection (or access to it) at his own institution inadequate for his needs. In the fall of 1968, Ohio discovered that students and faculty in forty-six academic institutions scattered throughout the state used off-campus libraries and that public libraries accounted for 71 per cent of that use. Libraries at other academic institutions accounted for a mere 22 per cent of outside library use.

The number of academic institutions served by a single public library can be staggering. One director of a public library in a New York suburban county recently estimated that he served students from *fifty* different colleges during any one-week period. Two colleges are located in the same geographical area his library serves, but the library is also used by students attending such major metropolitan institutions as New York University, Columbia, Hunter, and Fordham—all in New York City—and Rutgers, Fairleigh Dickinson, and Paterson State—in New Jersey.

A survey of users of the Detroit main library's reference and research facilities during two sample weeks in 1967 and 1968 showed that full-time students accounted for 64 per cent of total use. Forty-two per cent were college and university students; 22 per cent were noncollege, primarily high school students. These figures did not include the thousands of part-time students who also used the library during the survey period. Of particular interest was the discovery that an average of 60 per cent of all people who visited the library, regardless of primary occupation—whether they were accountants, lawyers, clerical workers, or what-have-you—came to the library for "schoolwork." Nurses, for example, gave this reason for using the public library in 50 per cent of their responses. Between 40 and 50 per cent of the accountants, clerical workers, musicians, and labor relations personnel gave "schoolwork" as the reason for their visits. Of all the twenty-seven occupational groups coded for the survey, only eight groups fell below 25 per cent in naming education as the reason for using the public library. Next to full-time students, teachers ranked highest in total use.

Studies in Colorado, New York, Ohio, and elsewhere indicate that the main reasons given by students for their use of off-campus libraries are (1) convenience, (2) depth and breadth of the collection, and (3) familiarity. A 1973 Colorado survey of high school, college, and university students found that of these groups, high school students were more likely to seek out a public library, and "usage of public libraries is not merely a matter of convenience but rather a preference among some students."

College and high school students tend to be fairly sophisticated library users. The Colorado study also found that students are generally more aware of library services, make more use of available library services, and feel more prone to use proposed new services than do nonstudents. Over four fifths of both levels of students borrowed books from their local public libraries and over two thirds used the reference section. Detailed reference work—such as using bibliographies or back issues of magazines—was reported by three fifths of the college students and about half of the secondary-school students. College-student use of public-library services included bibliographies, interlibrary loans, photocopy facilities, out-of-state newspapers, closed circuit TV rooms, microreproductions, special cultural programs, and public lectures.

PUBLIC LIBRARIES AND THE HIGH SCHOOL STUDENT

Why does a high school student use the public library?

For one thing, the public library is usually open after the school library closes. The public library is also available on weekends.

Mitchell Baron, a student at South Shore High School in Brooklyn, New York, puts it another way: "The school library doesn't have the stuff we need." (Many school libraries are primarily curriculum oriented and lack sufficient breadth to fulfill all the student's requirements.)

Then there are research projects like the one given to a member of an economics class in Mobile, Alabama, whose assignment was to compare today's prices for consumer goods with those of the 1930s and 1940s. He went to his public library and examined microfilm copies of *The New York Times* to compare clothing advertisements then and now. Members of the Needham, Massachusetts, high school class were assigned the task of writing a paper on the life of a well-known local historical figure. Their main source turned out to be the local newspaper archives in the public library.

Maybe the student is one of a group of teen-agers who gather at one of the big library tables to do homework with friends, especially if conditions are crowded at home.

And, of course, there are also the long-time users who started out in the children's reading room during preschool years and have kept up the habit of coming back for books, advice, and guidance ever since.

One or more of these reasons usually fits the millions of high school students who use America's public libraries every year.

PUBLIC LIBRARIES AND THE COLLEGE STUDENT

In addition to the once-typical college student home for vacation (who still jams his hometown public library during summers and holidays), there is now a fast-growing new breed of student who is a regular, year-round public-library user. He or she is the commuting student. He may go to school full time or part time, he may work or not work, his classes may be held off campus or on campus. None of these factors is as important to his pattern of library use as is the fact that he lives "off campus." Generally, he or she lives at home and the closest library is usually the public library. Even students enrolled at colleges or universities with exceptional library facilities will make substantial use of community public libraries for the sake of convenience.

Specialized book needs may force commuting students to use several different public-library collections. One full-time undergraduate majoring in classics at a Manhattan university found certain obscure publications that were unobtainable at his university library in the extensive collection of the New York Public Library. To obtain ordinary circulation items that were already borrowed from his university library or were on reserve and therefore not in circulation, he made use of various branch libraries around the city. As accompanist to his school glee club, he also consulted the city's Music Library.

Suburban commuting students are apt to follow even more complicated travel and studying patterns than their urban counterparts. Consider the student who lives with his family in Woodbourne (New York), works in Tuxedo Park (New York) as a professional teacher, and is taking a course at Paterson State (New Jersey) for his master's degree, and you have the hectic composite that is the commuting student. This student, according to Mrs. Matilda Gocek who examined him and others like him in four southeastern New York counties, will use the handiest library, but will be willing to library hop to locate the materials he needs. Nine times out of ten, the "handiest" library for the commuting student is the public library near his home.

Another primary factor influencing the pattern of library use by college students is the quality of the library collection at his institution of learning. According to a report recently issued by the National Commission on Libraries and Information Science, the institutional libraries of community colleges are severely understaffed, their collections are only "50 per cent of the indicated needs for collections for their enrollments and programs," and access to these libraries is limited by short hours of service. Of all the academic libraries found to fall short of the "minimum need" of sixty hours of library service a week, more than half are two-year colleges. Community colleges are the fastest growing sector in higher education, with an increase in enrollment of more than fivefold since 1960, and with anticipated continued growth at least into the early 1980s. What this means in terms of increasing dependence on public libraries by community-college students is self-evident.

PUBLIC LIBRARIES AND THE PART-TIME STUDENT

The most significant rise in student use of public libraries has resulted from the phenomenal growth in the number of adults enrolling in educational programs. For the first time in our history the majority of new students enrolled in postsecondary institutions, for both credit and noncredit work, are adult students continuing their education on a part-time basis. Part-time students have far outstripped increases in full-time enrollment. By 1980 their number is expected to have more than doubled over 1970 figures, accounting for 43 per cent of total college and university enrollment.

In 1959, one adult in eleven was involved in adult education. By 1973, one adult in four was involved with adult education, and one in eight was heading for a degree. These are the middle-management executives in their forties and fifties who feel the hot breath of competition from more academically qualified younger men; housewives who want to reenter the job market; mid-career job changers; and adults who had dropped out of college ten, twenty, thirty years ago and now simply want the satisfaction of "getting that degree."

These are highly motivated students who live off campus and tend to be keen learners, seeking extra reading in their fields, eager to pursue research for their school papers. Being a reference public librarian is a lot more challenging now that the adult student has joined the swelling ranks of regular public-library users.

PUBLIC LIBRARIES AND
THE INDEPENDENT LEARNER

Potentially the most revolutionary change in higher education within the last few years, and one offering the greatest challenge to public librarians, has been the growth in so-called nontraditional education. At least a hundred accredited institutions of higher learning offer different programs for such learners, and these and similar programs are increasing each year.

Although nontraditional education takes many forms, the emphasis is on nonclassroom study and independent learning. Programs are geared to working adults who frequently cannot find the time or money to pursue traditional classroom instruction. Most provide little or no teacher contact; little or no library facilities. The student's primary day-to-day help is likely to come from his public librarian.

Nontraditional programs leading toward recognized academic accreditation include:

1. *Proficiency examinations.* These allow students to earn full-course credit by examination without attending class. One of the best known is the College Level Examination Program (CLEP) initiated by the College Entrance Examination Board in the mid-1960s. CLEP tests are offered in more than fifty college subjects for which credit may be received at some eighteen hundred participating colleges and universities. Since 1971, over a million CLEP tests have been taken. It does not matter where, when, or how the student learned the subject matter, if the results of his test are acceptable to his college, he receives credit. Some institutions allow as many as sixty credits to be earned through proficiency examination. CLEP offers no preparation guidance to students.

2. *External degrees.* Over one hundred colleges and universities in thirty-nine states offer recognized external degrees designed to serve those who are, for whatever reason, unable to attend institutions of higher learning. Some colleges, such as Empire State in New York and Thomas A. Edison in New Jersey, have no faculty, no classrooms, and no libraries. Credits are often earned by a combination of means—proficiency examinations, televised instruction, regular courses, life experience that can be shown to be the equivalent of a college-level competence in a given area, noncollegiate sponsored instruction given by private companies such as Eastman Kodak or General Electric.

3. *Correspondence courses.* More than fifty-member colleges and universities of the National University Extension Association offer correspondence courses, ranging from accounting to writing, for which undergraduate credit is given; some seven institutions offer graduate credit by correspondence. These courses are designed for those who either want to or must study at home and prefer to work at their own pace.

The emphasis on self-preparation in all forms of nontraditional study means that library use by these students is bound to be far greater than that of traditional students. And the fact that these students live off campus obviously means that primary reliance will be on the community public library.

The Commission on Non-Traditional Study, a group of twenty-six educators headed by Samuel B. Gould, was formed in 1971 by the College Entrance Examination Board and the Educational Testing Service to examine the entire range of nontraditional study and to formulate specific recommendations for the future guidance of nontraditional education. In its 1973 report entitled *Diversity by Design,* the Commission recommended, "The public library should be strengthened to become a far more powerful instrument for nontraditional education than is now the case." The Commission urged college and university faculty members and administrators to work with public librarians in developing nontraditional study opportunities at the postsecondary level, pointing out that the public library's "vast capabilities have often been ignored."

MEETING STUDENT NEEDS

The public library fills the day-in and day-out needs of most undergraduates through its reference collection, its loan of circulating books, its interlibrary loan system.

Increasingly, libraries are undertaking to meet the challenge of providing special services to support the older student for whom the transition back to school may be difficult.

Joan Walsh, a mature woman with two of her children already in college, has been wanting to go back to college herself ever since she dropped out in her junior year to get married. College-degree courses offered at her local public library, a little more than a mile from her home in Port Washington, New York, have made it possible for her to do so. Another woman in the same program, already on her way to a better job, points out that she would not be working toward her degree if she had to travel to some university campus to attend classes.

Why the attraction of adult-education classes in the public library?

"It's a familiar place," explains Virginia Leipzig, student counselor at Adelphi, the university providing classes at Port Washington and in half a dozen other libraries on Long Island. "Many adults are really frightened by colleges. They're big. You always seem to walk into the wrong place. They don't know who you are. If you've ever been an adult student," she went on, "you'll remember the terror of those first classes. By going to the library you don't risk so much." Adelphi has found that after one or two courses at the library, most of these students are emboldened and, often with companions they have met in their classes, go on to further study on campus.

Hundreds of libraries across the country are cooperating in one way or another with nearby colleges to provide classrooms, equipment, and space for viewing course lectures on videotape, as well as providing backup study materials.

A joint effort of the Chicago Public Library and the City Colleges of Chicago allows students to pursue courses for credit in six different city libraries. Students can do all their required work, including consultations with faculty and counselors, in the public library. The method of study uses video and audio cassettes in conjunction with texts, study guides, and a library full of related readings. A recent innovation is a newspaper course of study offered by the University of California Extension, San Diego. Lectures are published weekly in the local press and students are graded on papers they prepare after reading each lecture. The library's role in the program is, in the words of the director of the City Colleges, Les Sandy, to provide a " 'community of learning' where students coming into the library are known and feel welcomed and free to ask for assistance when they need it, and to settle down and study when they don't. Where librarians with genuine interest in the students' progress provide the encouragement to the people studying outside of traditional tracks." The program provides a simple, unstructured, and inexpensive way to start college. Texts and study guides are available in each participating library. Each student is assigned two viewing hours a week at the most convenient time for him. If he comes, he is assured of time at the video player; if he does not, no one gets upset. The program aims to help mature students through their first two years of college as quickly as possible so that they can pursue their objectives in a four-year college. Since its inception in 1973, more than a thousand adults have pursued the program.

In addition to the college-credit courses, the joint program also helps students prepare for high school equivalency examinations and CLEP examinations or simply those who seek personal enrichment. Taken as a whole, the program has attracted such groups as: mature people over thirty with little or no formal education; people well educated in another tongue but who are weak in English; young people who have been in correctional institutions, or are on welfare, or who have had their education interrupted for one reason or another; those already in college who want to squeeze in additional courses.

Both the St. Louis Public Library and the St. Louis County Library cooperate with the innovative University of Mid-America, a consortium of state universities in Missouri, Kansas, Nebraska, and Iowa, which offers college credit through home study, intensive reading and discussion at the libraries or other learning centers supplemented by television. The St. Louis Public Library, for example, has three courses on video cassettes. The University of Mid-America lends the library a video-cassette machine and TV as well as all the course materials. The library has these set aside in a special room so that anyone enrolled in the program can come to watch on TV and do his work at any time when the library is open.

St. Louis, like a number of other libraries, offers a course in how to use the library. Classes meet Saturday mornings for eight weeks and are, of course, free. Such courses are a direct response to the needs of adult students, particularly those participating in nontraditional programs.

Increasingly, public libraries make a point of stocking their shelves with books called for in proficiency examination study guides. Many stock a variety of textbooks helpful in preparation for CLEP examinations. A few libraries, such as Dallas Public Library, prepare special study guides for independent learners. And St. Louis Public Library actually administers CLEP examinations and those of the American College Testing Proficiency Examination Program, in addition to providing guidance and preparation resources for these students.

EDUCATIONAL ADVISORY SERVICES

Servicing the needs of the individual user has always been a primary function of the public library. As an aid to those looking for courses in a particular field or attempting to choose a college or university, public libraries have traditionally given shelf space to school catalogues and directories. Today that is not enough. The spectacular growth in adult education and the great diversity of programs that have sprung up around the country within the past decade—many of them programs designed to give mature adults an opportunity to acquire academic credentials outside traditional forms of higher education—means that potential students are very much in need of guidance from a neutral source in their communities.

Many of the anxieties of the prospective nontraditional student can be allayed by simply being told the facts. Many adults worry about the consequences of having failed a freshman course ten years before, or having attended a nonacademic high school, or not having graduated from high school at all. Librarians who serve as educational advisers can reassure such individuals that none of these things matter.

Numerous studies have shown that there are literally millions of people who would like to continue their education but have no idea of the opportunities available to them. In response to this need, public libraries are expanding their activities to provide learner's advisory services. As the Commission on Non-Traditional Learning points out, "the public library is probably the best community agency to house, staff, and maintain a full guidance and counseling center."

One of the newest programs is the experimental Higher Educational Library Advisory Service (HELAS) being offered at four libraries in New York State in conjunction with the New York State

Board of Regents because, explains Pat Dyer, Board of Regents director of the project, "The public library is truly the all-round educational center for adults, particularly the person who wants to explore a number of educational options." Under this program librarians are specially trained to give information on all types of postsecondary-education options available in the community, to help individuals in making decisions related to their educational goals, and to refer people to appropriate institutions.

HELAS librarians are also seeing many clients who are using the library for the first time. The Queens Borough (New York) Public Library HELAS program has attracted many minority-group members, including recent immigrants from Jamaica and Haiti. One of the library's most impressive student users is a Haitian mother of five children who holds down a full-time job while earning her required credits for a degree in nursing through the Board of Regent's External Degree examinations. "She has been taking a minimum of two exams every three months," explains Kay Cavanaugh, the HELAS librarian who works with her, "and she has been passing them with flying colors."

In the early 1970s, special emphasis was given to learner's advisory services in a number of public libraries across the country—Atlanta, Denver, Baltimore, Miami, Portland (Maine), Salt Lake City, St. Louis, Tulsa, and Woodbridge (New Jersey). Special library programs offered in-depth advisory and information-support services to adults interested in learning outside of a formal educational setting. The chief element that distinguished the independent learner project from traditionally offered services was the extended staff involvement with the individual learner throughout his learning project. "People often need help in deciding exactly what it is they want to learn," explains Edwin Beckerman, director of the Woodbridge Public Library, "and they need help in clarifying their ambitions. This is the job of the learning advisers."

Mr. Beckerman explains the function of learner's advisory services with a graphic example.

A man, for instance, asked for a book on air conditioning. The normal procedure would be to direct him to the area where he would find a book on the subject. In an interview conducted by a learning adviser, we learned that the man was interested in the technical aspects of repairing air-conditioners and wanted to become a licensed technician. We tailor-made a program geared to his needs.

Programs like these underscore the increasing importance of the public library as an independent community learning center.

SHORTCHANGING THE PUBLIC LIBRARIES

"[E]ducation is but a key to open the doors of libraries."
—André Maurois

Although public libraries have been playing an ever-increasing role in the educational system of this country, they have received short shrift in federal and state budgets.

The National Center for Education Statistics estimates that $81.4 billion federal, state, and local tax dollars were spent in 1974–75 by the nation's elementary and secondary schools and institutions of higher learning. In contrast, the total amount of tax dollars spent in 1974 on public libraries amounted to approximately $1 billion, the equivalent of 1.2 per cent of the education budget.

Higher education alone accounts for $19.7 billion of the total tax dollars spent on education, or $2,525 per full-time equivalent student. Operating expenditures in 1974 by college and university libraries amounted to an average of *$134 per student.*

In marked contrast, public-library tax funds allocable to college students in the 1974 population on a per capita basis amounted to only $40 million, or *$5.15 per full-time equivalent student.*

When it comes to the source of tax dollars, *91 per cent* ($17.9 billion) of the tax dollars spent by institutions of higher education comes from federal and state government sources, while only *16.7 per cent* ($168 million) of the funds for public libraries comes from the same sources. (A detailed state-by-state breakdown of student library expenditures is set forth in Appendix B.)

The importance attached to providing student library services is reflected in the following sample of library expenditures by major publicly funded institutions of higher education and the per capita allocation to full-time equivalent student enrollments in 1974–75:

	TOTAL LIBRARY EXPENDITURES	NUMBER OF STUDENTS	PER STUDENT LIBRARY EXPENDITURES
University of California	$42,272,000	129,110	$327
University of Texas	$12,586,000	72,581	$173
University of the State of New York	$33,569,000	224,335	$150

The *annual* library expenditures by these *three* institutions alone *exceed the total spent by the federal government* for public-library support in all fifty states.

Nobody would argue for a reduction in the allocation of funds for college and university libraries. Indeed, the National Commission on Libraries and Information Science study, *National Inventory of Library Needs—1975,* underscores the need for upgrading academic libraries, particularly at two-year institutions. The point is that the federal and state governments have sorely neglected their obligations to public libraries, viewed from the vantage point of education alone.

The enormous increase in higher education in this country means that public libraries are now more frequently and intensively used by students than ever before. Pauline Winnick of the U.S. Office of Education recently pointed out that "The public library gets the brunt of whatever is happening in an educational sense in the entire community. Whatever program in education may be introduced with any effect—the library feels it. It may not be prepared to handle it, but they get the impact."

The most direct result from the shortchanging of public libraries is a restriction on the hours when libraries are open. For part-time and commuting students, a closed library door often means complete denial of access to library materials. Even for full-time students the need for extended-hour library operations is real. Classes, sports, and extracurricular activities occupy much, if not most, of the "normal" hours of library operation. Student need for libraries is especially heavy in the evenings, holidays, and weekends. These are the first hours eliminated when cutbacks in public-library service occur, to avoid overtime and other added costs associated with night and weekend use.

The most recent national figures available (1975 for college and university libraries, 1974 for public libraries) show that campus libraries are open for use an average of eighty-two hours per week per student, an average in excess of the sixty-hour-a-week minimum for academic libraries indicated in *National Inventory of Library Needs—1975*. In marked contrast, half the population served by public libraries has library access for fewer hours than the indicated minimum of sixty-six hours per week for libraries serving more than twenty-five thousand people and forty-five hours per week in smaller communities. Who is hurt most by this sharp difference in library hours?

——The *commuting student* and the *part-time student* who often must work during the day and study at night and on weekends.

——The *independent, nontraditional learner* who usually has no convenient institutional library and is thrown on public-library resources.

——The *full-time student* who finds his or her own institutional library inadequate or inconvenient.

Sharp budget cuts, accompanied by inflationary cost increases, have had a devastating effect on public-library hours in the past several years. While we have given heavy support to campus-related student library services, students who must depend on public-library resources are being cheated by shortsighted governmental funding, particularly on the federal and state levels.

CHAPTER 4 ✻✻✻✻✻✻✻✻✻✻✻✻✻✻✻✻✻✻✻✻✻✻✻✻✻✻✻✻✻✻✻✻✻✻✻✻✻

Creating Jobs and Helping the Jobseeker

Martin Radtke could neither read nor write when he arrived at Ellis Island in 1913 at the age of thirty. He was just another penniless young man from Lithuania who had come to the land of opportunity to seek his fortune.

He found it at the public library.

Radtke taught himself to read and began devouring every business magazine and economics text the public library had to offer. He adopted a habit of going to the public library three times a week, a pattern which he kept up until the day he died. Employing the information gained at the library, Radtke accumulated $1 million in the stock market. When he died he left his entire estate to the New York Public Library.

> I had little opportunity for formal education as a young man in Lithuania, and am deeply indebted to the New York Public Library for the opportunity to educate myself. In appreciation, I have given the library my estate with the wish that it be used so that others can have the same opportunity made available to me.

Countless Americans owe their careers directly or indirectly to our public libraries: Technical research may have helped to create their jobs; reference materials may have guided their career choices or helped prepare them for job applications; library materials may have provided job advancement; business services may have kept their employers afloat. Whatever the means, the fact is that our public libraries play a little-known but major role in the American economy and job market.

To understand the special place of the public library in our country's economy it is important to understand some basic facts about our employment patterns:

——The average working American looks for a new job every two to three years.

——The average working American changes careers three to five times in his lifetime.

——Each year at least twenty million working Americans are out of work for an average period of seventy days.

——For every 1 per cent increase in national unemployment, the federal government loses $16 billion—$14 billion from reduced tax revenues and $2 billion paid out in unemployment aid.

This is the setting in which the public libraries function. Increasingly, they have demonstrated a major potential for aiding the country's working population, through job information centers, helping people advance in their careers, and by aiding in the creation of new jobs and protection of existing ones.

JOB INFORMATION CENTERS

In 1972, the Manpower Administration of the U.S. Department of Labor gave a demonstration grant to the Yonkers (New York) Public Library to test the idea of establishing Job Information Centers at public libraries located in a high unemployment area. Reference librarian Nancy Johmann was given the job of setting up the center. Ms. Johmann approached the task as a jobseeker herself, collecting all the data she would want if she were hunting for a job.

The first thing Ms. Johmann did was the obvious: She put together in one place all of the library's books, pamphlets, and journals that might be helpful in finding jobs. Then she set up a bulletin board with a daily display of classified help-wanted ads from all of the area's newspapers. Each day she sent a staff member to pick up a microfiche copy of the listings of job opportunities included in the New York State Employment Service Job Banks. She also posted all city, county, state, and federal civil-service announcements. She developed a cooperative working relationship with nineteen nearby private employment agencies covering every imaginable area of employment—managerial, professional, clerical, and office skills, unskilled labor, factory work, administrative, technical, domestic, health, temporary jobs, and jobs for the handicapped. Job openings from local businesses were obtained and displayed on 3 by 5 cards tacked up on the bulletin boards. Job listings were updated weekly.

The new Job Information Center also compiled a file of relevant community agencies and organizations such as the Education Opportunities Center, Yonkers Career Center, Women's Center of Yonkers, the Employment Resource Center—organizations that have employment programs for special groups such as young adults, disadvantaged, veterans, handicapped, retarded, senior citizens, and apprenticeship and intern programs. Ms. Johmann subscribed to specialized newsletters and periodicals—*Ad Search,* a weekly service listing nationwide job openings; *Affirmative Action Register,* a monthly national listing of jobs for female, minority, and handicapped persons; the *Chronicle for Higher Education,* listing a broad range of jobs in that field.

An important function of the Job Information Center was constant scanning of literature for new and better materials and for articles of special interest to be tacked up on the boards. Special publications produced by the Job Center were a natural spin-off. The first of these, "Your Job and Your Future," included a list of employment agencies in the area keyed to the types of positions in which each specialized, a particularly useful compilation, as it was the only verified list in print.

During its first fifteen months of operation the Yonkers Job Information Center served close to eleven thousand patrons and initiated almost seven thousand referrals to various employment-related agencies. The center was so successful in fulfilling its mission as a clearinghouse for job information that today it has served as the prototype for a network of some forty Job Information Centers in New York State, most of them at least partially funded under the Library Services and Construction Act.

The job centers do not offer an employment service—they do not match jobs and applicants—but rather, they are designed to help overcome many of the informational problems associated with the job-search process. One of the best of the centers was set up in 1975 in the Hempstead (New York) Public Library, a bright and cheerful, low, red brick structure situated on a greensward in close proximity to the mayor's office, the police department, the labor department, the Chamber of Commerce, and other agencies with which the library coordinates its job information activities. Here the emphasis is very much on rendering personal assistance to the unemployed individual. Says director Elsie Duszkiewicz, "Our most important ingredient in that center is a staff member, a professional librarian. . . . Many of these people have never been inside a library and they don't realize what is there for them." It is the responsibility of the job center librarian to know the full resources of the library and to know the community as well. Thus, if a woman who comes in for job help is accompanied by her husband who is a functional illiterate, she not only gets her job information, but he is gently steered into the tutoring program of the local Literacy Volunteers of America (which also has its headquarters in the library). Jobless people who are unaware that they are entitled to government assistance programs, such as food stamps, are directed to the librarian in charge of social-service information. The library works hard to maintain the quality of its referrals to other agencies. People are given the names of individuals with whom the library has an established relationship at the agency to which the center refers them. Before a job hunter is sent over to see Mrs. Muriel Green at the CETA program, for example, the librarian takes pains to explain to him or her what the program is and how to qualify for it. The job center provides a variety of support services. Career counseling at the library is arranged through the county's Office of Women's Services. Learner's advisory services are also provided.

Workshops are a regular activity of the Hempstead center. A baby-sitters' workshop was of help in the spring of 1978 for youngsters who wanted to earn money but who were unable to qualify for the Neighborhood Youth Corps or other special programs. The National Alliance of Minority Businessmen joined the library in sponsoring a program on "How to Get a Summer Job." One of the best-attended workshops was devoted to "The Joys and Pitfalls of Starting Your Own Business."

Job Information Centers are still in their infancy, but their potential for providing what the country badly lacks—a national job information service program—is very real and exciting.

CAREER CHANGE AND ADVANCEMENT

"I visit the library about once a week, and one day I saw this flyer about a workshop on the 'ABC of job hunting,'" recalls Anna Wieland, a thirty-nine-year-old Puerto Rican mother of three young girls. The workshop, organized by the Job Information Center at the Yonkers Public Library, gave Mrs. Wieland, who had been out of the job market for ten years, useful tips on rewriting her resume, and how to conduct herself in an employment interview, but most of all, she said later, "It built up my confidence . . . being out for all those years, I began to feel maybe there's nothing out there for me." Mrs. Wieland had no trouble landing the job she wanted.

A Marine Corps Vietnam War veteran, with a wife and two small children, was hospitalized for two years after suffering a nervous breakdown because of the strain of running his own business. While still an outpatient at the Veterans Hospital he turned to the Hempstead Public Library's Job Information Center for help in finding a new field he could work in with less stress. The librarian arranged for him to receive career counseling and testing at the library. Then through a referral from the Job Information Center he obtained a new job as a guide in one of the county's historical museums, where his love of history serves him well. He is back with his family and is doing well.

A Brooklyn woman who had been working as a therapist for twenty-three years wanted to obtain state certification as a full-fledged occupational therapist. Her librarian suggested courses to supplement her career background in preparation for an upcoming state exam; recommended three schools in the area offering such classes; prepared a suggested reading list of the subject; and referred the applicant to the Civil Service Commission for more detailed information. With this help the candidate succeeded.

In Massachusetts, a young woman who had been unable to find work since she graduated with a teacher's certificate eight months earlier recently spent an hour picking out a new career on the computer terminal located in the Lawrence Public Library. The computer presented her with a questionnaire which evaluated what other kinds of work she might be suited for, then gave her a description of the background of the average person in fields that interested her, a description of what is done on a daily basis in those occupations, and a rundown on wage scales. It also gave her both statewide and regional forecasts of the numbers of jobs opening up in these fields. After she chose one of the new occupations, the computer listed schools in the northeast where training in that occupation was offered and provided her with the name of the director, the tuition, entrance requirements, whether there was a placement service there, and information about financial aid. The computer then supplied her with a printout of the information to take home with her for future reference.

These examples give some idea of how public libraries can effectively supply career-counseling information to help people with career changes and advancement. Although the programs they represent are in their infancy, the need for such services across the country is increasingly acute.

At any given time, approximately six to seven million people are looking for new jobs without success. In recent years, young people and emancipated women have been moving into the labor market in greater numbers than the U.S. economy has been able to absorb. There are simply not enough jobs to go around. Economists do not hold out much hope for any substantial easing of the tight job market for a number of years to come. A significant part of the unemployment problem is not due to a shortage of jobs, but to a failure to match job applicants and job openings. The United States has no organized national program to help applicants find and land suitable jobs—particularly jobs that are open and waiting to be filled. Richard Lathrop, director of the National Center for Job-Market Studies, points out that by reducing the average time taken to find employment by only four days—from seventy to sixty-six days—the annual count of people without jobs would drop by one million. Closing that gap alone could save the nation billions of dollars in lost output.

A recent survey directed by Soloman Arbeiter of the College Entrance Examination Board found that over one third (36 per cent) of all adults (sixteen to sixty-five years old and not in school full time) are either making or anticipating job or career changes. These forty million "in-transition" adults want career services of all types, the study found, but they are most interested in information services, particularly specific information on jobs, careers, or educational opportunities. Mr. Arbeiter expects the in-transition population to increase in view of the continued lowering of sex and race barriers and elimination of other artificial barriers to employment, including educational and credential requirements not related to job performance. The study identifies the in-transition adults as being predominantly female, white, between twenty and thirty-nine years of age, married with one to three children living in the household, and with family incomes of ten thousand dollars a year or more. Most adults in transition are presently employed and wish to either change fields or to change the level or status in their present fields, primarily because of financial need, but also because of a desire to seek more interesting work and to advance professionally.

Respondents in the CEEB study on career changing listed the following as the top ten career information services they needed:

  lists of available jobs;
  facts on occupational fields;
  career possibilities and the most rapid path for advancement;
  educational programs;
  job skills training;

relationship of special abilities and strengths to various types of jobs;

financial aid sources;

educational programs offered at different schools;

which schools could best meet personal needs;

facts on how personal abilities relate to educational success.

It is precisely these kinds of information that public libraries have demonstrated they can provide, either directly or by working in cooperation with other agencies.

Actually, there is nothing new about the role of public libraries in helping people with career counseling and advancement. What is changing is the concentration of specific career development data and the utilization of more sophisticated techniques for putting them to use. Writers of books on employment have long been directing their readers to the resources of the public library. Richard Lathrop, author of *Who's Hiring Who,* directs job hunters to go to their public libraries and "tell your librarian the occupational field you are exploring. Be specific in naming the kind of enterprise you want to enter. Ask to be led to the pertinent references, periodicals, and directories that will give you the best information on the occupation, companies, products, and officials that are targets in your job search." Standard library reference materials that might be used in a job search include corporate annual reports and industrial, trade, or professional directories which provide names and addresses of potential employers. (A present White House correspondent for the Associated Press landed her first job by mailing off resumes to all eastern seaboard newspapers from just such a directory she found at her public library.) Career-guidance materials in most public libraries include information about resume writing, occupations and careers, planning and carrying out a job search, employment agencies and employers, occupational and vocational training, how to start and run your own business. There are books and pamphlets that answer questions about overseas employment, summer jobs, general job-market information from other states, volunteer opportunities. Job openings can also be hunted up in the pages of local and out-of-town newspapers and in the classified sections of magazines in specialized areas such as accounting, engineering, management. Educational opportunities to sharpen skills or attain credentials for a leg up in job status can be found in a wide variety of reference sources.

Another traditional career assistance role of public libraries is helping people prepare for state licensing examinations. There are approximately five hundred professional and nonprofessional occupations currently licensed by one or more states, and a number of others (such as able seaman) regulated by federal government agencies. The growing trend is to regulate more and more skilled and semiskilled occupations. Written examinations are required for many state licenses. Public libraries are readily available sources of published preparation materials—frequently including questions and answers from previous licensing examinations. Representative occupations requiring written licensing examinations in various jurisdictions include accountants, auto mechanics, cosmetologists, dental hygienists, dispensing opticians, electricians, pharmacists, practical nurses, land surveyors, life insurance agents, private investigators, real estate salesmen, and scores of others.

Many public libraries also post notices of upcoming civil-service examinations and supply information about civil-service job opportunities in scores of fields. Government employment has been expanding faster than any other industry and is expected to remain a major source of new jobs through the mid-1980s. An estimated eight to fifteen million people prepare each year for a multitude of different civil-service examinations from air-traffic controllers to bank examiners to post-office clerks. Arco Publishing Company, the leading publisher of civil-service preparation manuals, estimates that 50 per cent of its sales go to public libraries. While thousands of libraries stock these manuals on a selective basis, they are in such heavy demand that some two hundred libraries have standing orders for each new edition of a civil-service manual as it comes off the presses. At least one library (Detroit) also sells these books as a convenience to users who wish to purchase them.

Difficult economic times increase the number of public-library users seeking career and job information. This natural phenomenon was noted by Bernard Berelson in his classic study of library use, *The Library's Public*. Berelson noted that during the Great Depression of the 1930s fully 80 to 85 per cent of library patrons used the readers' advisory services of the public library either through a desire to advance in their occupations or for self-improvement. As the American economy has grown more and more industrialized in the subsequent half century, slight swings in the economy have exerted heavy pressures on the employment market and in turn on the public library. The increasing complexity of job requirements has also increased the challenge to come up with new techniques to supplement the traditional source of career materials found on the library shelves.

The most promising of the new career-counseling techniques is the flow of job information made possible by computer technology. In Massachusetts, the placing of computer terminals in public libraries has been paid for by the local Comprehensive Employment and Training Act (CETA) office which uses the interactive computer along with other types of career counseling in their employment training program for disadvantaged, unemployed, and underemployed individuals of all ages. The occupational information is developed by the Massachusetts Occupational Information Service (MOIS) under a demonstration grant from the U.S. Department of Labor's National Occupation Information Service, which has similar demonstration programs in seven other states. The program is geared to providing current, locally relevant information to aid people, especially students and out-of-work youth, in the process of choosing jobs and careers. The system includes information on some 265 occupations representing about 95 per cent of Massachusetts employment.

Peter Vanier, head of the $20 million CETA program in the Greater Lawrence Area in Massachusetts, is convinced that placing the terminals in public libraries was one of his better ideas. Not only are libraries usually centrally located, on bus routes, and with excellent access for handicapped, he points out, but their services are available evenings and on weekends, as well as during normal business hours. Vanier also wanted job applicants to have the experience of going to the library. "People are going to have to go seek out information, just like they have to seek out jobs and services," he says. "They've got to be mobile, so we felt it was important for us to provide the service but we didn't want to place it on their doorstep. A lot of younger kids will just use the library to get out of the rain, and this program gives them a reason to go there, to see the resources that are available there, to see other people studying, reading, and inquiring."

At the Lawrence Public Library, the computer terminal is located right in the middle of things at the reference desk. "It meets a very definite need," explains James Kennedy, the library's director, "using about a dozen books you could come up with about the same information, but the kind of person who would use the terminal because of the novelty or because they're not necessarily linear readers, would not dig into the twelve or fourteen books." Nevertheless, the librarian has made a point of displaying books on career selection and job hunting in the same area to encourage CETA people and others using the terminal to also start thinking in terms of using books to find out career and other information that can help them. Providing job-related materials, after all, is only one of the valuable services the public library has to offer.

THE PUBLIC LIBRARY AS EMPLOYER

There is no public institution in America to compare with the public library when it comes to providing jobs for students and others who need part-time employment. A recent special study on library manpower by the Bureau of Labor Statistics reports a dramatic rise in part-time library jobs. An estimated 120,000 persons worked as library attendants and assistants in 1970 compared to 37,000 in 1960. This is an annual average increase of 12.5 per cent. Approximately two additional library attendants and assistants took jobs for each librarian added to the labor force during the 1960s. For the most part, the increase is attributable to greater use of nonprofessionals in library work to perform work once done by professionals.

More than one third of the 120,000 attendants and assistants worked in public libraries, and another one third worked in aca-

demic libraries. School libraries, though predominant in employment of full-time librarians, employed only 16 per cent of all attendants and assistants. Special libraries employed some 13 per
cent of the total.

Part-time employment is very high in library occupations. In
1970, one out of every three librarians worked part time (that is,
fewer than thirty-five hours a week), as did roughly two out of
three library attendants and assistants, according to data from the
1970 census on number of hours worked.

> Part-time employment seems to be more significant in librar-
> ianship than in many other occupations. For professional, techni-
> cal, and kindred workers as a whole, about 20 per cent worked
> part-time in 1970, compared to 34 per cent of the librarians. And
> on the nonprofessional level, about 2 per cent of all clerical
> workers were employed part-time in 1970, compared to nearly 63
> per cent of the library attendants and assistants.

Many public officials, executives, and professionals who occupy
positions of responsibility worked their way through college with a
library job. Many of tomorrow's leaders are working at part-time
jobs in public libraries today. The growing threat to library survival because of rising costs threatens the survival of these special
job opportunities. Experience in cities which have been forced to
cut library services demonstrated that part-time employees, being
junior in point of service, are usually the first to be terminated.

HELPING TO CREATE NEW JOBS

When Robert Hutchings Goddard was a boy growing up in
Worcester, Massachusetts, he fell far behind his schoolmates at
the local high school because of recurrent bouts of colds, pleurisy,
and bronchitis. He tried to catch up by reading science books borrowed from the Worcester Public Library. He devoured textbooks
on electricity, chemistry, and the atmosphere. He also engaged in
his own brand of scientific experiments in the family attic.

One day, after studying a library book on the evolution of diamonds from carbon, sixteen-year-old Robert decided to try out his own theory on how to make diamonds. In his diary he wrote:

> I decided to heat some graphite in a small mass of iron by an oxy-hydrogen flame, and dump the mass into water, subsequently examining it for possible diamonds.

During the course of the experiment, the young scientist thrust a glass tube filled with hydrogen into the flame of his alcohol lamp, causing an explosion which drove particles of glass into the ceiling and through the attic doorway.

Goddard's biographer then picks up the tale:

> Startled by the explosion, their servant girl screamed out that she had been killed. The family calmly assured her that she was not, and pledged Robert to refrain from the manufacture of diamonds.

Blocked in his pursuit of quick riches through chemistry, young Goddard went back to his library books for other ideas. He continued to read whatever he could lay his hands on in the field of physics and science.

The following year, while taking a break from his self-imposed schedule of studies, he climbed the cherry tree in the back yard one day and stared off into space. There he imagined ". . . how wonderful it would be to make some device which had even the possibility of ascending to Mars." Thus began a fascination with the idea of space flight which led Goddard later to become the father of the space age. His subsequent experiments with acceleration and deceleration and the thrust of different fuels (many of them no less dangerous than trying to manufacture diamonds) led in time to the world's first flight of a liquid-propelled rocket engine on his Aunt Effie's farm in Auburn, Massachusetts, on March 16, 1926. His later experiments on the open ranges at Roswell, New Mexico, developed the prototypes for the rockets which were later to carry American astronauts beyond the realms of any young boy's imaginings—and to provide investments of billions of dollars and new jobs in a whole new field for tens of thousands of Americans.

The space industry is only one of the modern fields in which a major addition to the American economy has sprung from the thinking of an inventor who drew his basic ideas from visits to the public library.

Dr. Chester Carlson, the inventor of xerography, the basis for one of the largest new industries created by technology since World War II, spent hours of his time over many months reviewing literature in the New York Public Library. As Carlson explained it: "Things don't come to mind readily all of a sudden, like pulling things out of the air. You have to get your inspiration from somewhere and usually you get it from reading something else." Xerox Corporation, built on Dr. Carlson's invention, now directly employs some ninety-three thousand people, and its products indirectly provide jobs for hundreds of thousands more in offices throughout the country.

Dr. Edwin H. Land, inventor of the first practical synthetic light polarizing sheet and the "Land" camera, and founder of Polaroid Corporation, depended on the resources of the New York Public Library for much of his research in developing "instant photography."

Lee De Forest, one of America's great inventors—a pioneer in the development of radio, sound pictures, and television—in a letter written in 1958 to William S. Budington, director of the John Crerar Library in Chicago, said that "It was as a result of my hours spent at Crerar Library that I came across a German reference to a recent discovery by a German scientist by the name of Aschinass which gave me a greatly desired lead to a series of experiments which resulted in a somewhat reliable electrolytic detector of wireless telegraph signals. Had it not been for the delightful hours I spent at Crerar Library, I should never have come across that initial idea which meant so much to me during the next succeeding years. . . ." De Forest's investigations helped spark America's huge electronics industry.

Charles F. Burgess, developer of the dry cell (Burgess) battery, was also a Crerar Library user. In his biography, Alexander McQueen described two loose scraps of paper found in one of Burgess' notebooks. "One of them was a penciled list, in Burgess' handwriting, of cash assets. The total was important and therefore interesting. But it should be considered in relation to the other scrap of paper, which happened to be a blank book-call slip of the John Crerar Library, Chicago. The two pieces of paper were symbolic; the library slip stood for research, the cash assets stood for the results of research."

Jobs do not depend solely on the genius of such inventors, of course. Many jobs also depend on the continuation of existing trade, commerce, and manufacture in fields which are as old as the wheel. But few American businesses can survive for long without some attention to continuing research in fields such as technology, marketing, management, finance. What most people do not know is that in major employment centers, the public library plays a major role in helping with this research.

SCIENCE AND TECHNOLOGY

Twenty-three million Americans—well over a fourth of all jobholders—are employed by goods-producing industries. Overwhelmingly, these industries are based on knowledge derived from science and technology. Because science and engineering are built largely on the published records of earlier work done throughout the world, libraries play a vital role in helping these industries get started and grow.

More than sixty public libraries in the United States have special collections devoted to science and technology. What this resource means to goods-producing industries was graphically outlined at "The President's 1957 Conference on Technical and Distribution Research for the Benefit of Small Business" by Daniel Pfoutz, head of the Science and Technology Department of the Carnegie Library in Pittsburgh. Mr. Pfoutz described six case histories, of which this is an example:

> The salt domes of Louisiana are far removed from Pittsburgh, but one of our local engineering firms wanted to determine what had been done previously about mining techniques in the salt domes. They were interested in appraising the domes and determining their characteristics in order to approach the proper mining techniques.

The Library's role was to conduct a broad search of the literature to find what was known about the domes and what had been written about mining methods.

The public library set about the task of pulling together data to aid in the development of an exploratory drilling technique. The librarian drew on special reference and research tools such as topographic maps; U.S. Government research reports; International Catalogue of Scientific Literature; annotated Bibliography of Economic Geology; Bibliography of North American Geology; and Geophysical Abstracts and other publications issued by the Bureau of Mines. Later, Mr. Pfoutz could boast:

At the present time, they are sinking shafts and beginning mining operations.

A clear example of how information provided by a public library can help generate jobs. Mr. Pfoutz added simply, "This is what we do each day, all day long, at the Carnegie Library. That's the reason for our existing."

A more recent example from the Carnegie Library—1975—involved helping engineers plan for the manufacturing of briquets from bituminous coal dust. The library supplied a bibliography containing articles on techniques, cost, and various yearly production statistics.

Public libraries account for fifteen of the twenty-two U.S. patent depository collections, and their collections often include the many thousands of technical reports issued each year by the federal government, reports from NASA, the Atomic Energy Commission, and the Department of Defense. Professional and scientific journals, as well as other serial publications, usually provide the greatest strength of a science and technology collection. These publications offer advance information and discussion and the detailed records that support most scientific study. In chemistry, for example, about 93 per cent of everything published appears in journals.

The increase in numbers of new scientific and technical journals continues to soar. In 1960, *Chemical Abstracts* abstracted and indexed eight thousand journals; today they work with fourteen thousand. The torrent of scientific literature is such that although many special libraries are maintained by industry, "No company library," to quote an official of the General Electric Company, "can have on its shelves all the technical data . . . to supply the desired information on any one subject." That is why the public library is such an important part of the process.

Most of the sixty-plus public libraries with science-technology departments maintain special holdings keyed to the needs of local industry. Southern California's defense-contract industries are served by the San Diego Public Library's space and aeronautic collections; Houston Public Library has special petroleum geology collections, including drillers' logs and electric well logs for the Gulf Coast area; the public library in Toledo, where glassmaking is an important industry, has a special collection on glass and glass technology; Detroit Public Library, which serves the automobile manufacturing industry, places particular emphasis on metalworking, mechanical engineering, and allied subjects.

Much specialized technical information is now available in computer data banks. In West Virginia, business and industry (as well as other users) can tap into a free statewide on-line, computerized information retrieval service to learn about anything from coal gasification in South Africa to methods of employee training to whether or not a new paint formula has already been patented. The service is provided by the West Virginia Library Commission.

MANAGEMENT AND FINANCE

Most large corporations maintain their own special libraries, although they still depend on public libraries for backup information in fields outside their own areas of operation. It is the small businessman and individual entrepreneur who cannot afford the information tools necessary to set up or run his operation, and may even not know of their existence, who is the prime beneficiary of public-library resources in the fields of business management and finance.

According to the United States Small Business Administration, there are some nine million small businesses in this country. They comprise 95 per cent of all businesses in the United States and employ well over half (53 per cent) of those who work in private industry. As far back as the 1950s, the Small Business Administration began providing bibliographies to sources of information in public libraries for the use of small businessmen. SBA publications continue to encourage small businesses to take advantage of public-library facilities, pointing out to the small manufacturer, for example, that he can:

——Locate the names and addresses of prospective buyers around the world.

——Keep in touch with the newest patents in his field.

——Consult directories of all sorts.

——Use the talents of government specialists on hundreds of subjects from new products to business retirement.

——Read up on existing local, state, and federal laws as well as pending legislation.

——Obtain the free services of researchers to help him through the ever-growing maze of government and technical information.

Recognizing the businessman's need for quick information, many public libraries offer a special telephone reference service for businesses. (Among the best known of these is maintained by Sylvia Mechanic, business librarian at the Brooklyn Public Library, who receives calls from business firms all over the country. When Brooklyn's funds were slashed in 1975, business firms helped pick up the costs of keeping the service running.)

Some libraries—Cleveland, Dallas, Denver, Newark, Omaha, and Tulsa, for example—prepare and distribute business newsletters to library users who request them, which typically list new acquisitions, provide bibliographies on timely business subjects, and describe special features of the business division.

In 1961, the Bureau of Business Research of the University of Colorado prepared a study of the management tools available to public libraries to fill the informational needs of the small businessman. "Public Libraries," it noted, "are primary points of distribution for much material that otherwise would not be conveniently available to the small businessman." The study gave the following description of the way a properly equipped and staffed public library serves the business community (based on the Business and Technology Department of the Cleveland Public Library):

Here may be found an impressive and significant collection of business, scientific and trade journals, abstracting and indexing services, industrial and financial directories, market analyses, consumer buying habit studies, corporation reports, Government agency publications, business and financial newspapers and thousands of books on scientific, technical and business subjects.

Important as these resources are, they would be as a piece of intricate mechanical equipment without an operator, were it not for a trained, qualified staff standing ready to help extract the one fact, the pertinent bit of information, the exactly right book, report or magazine article needed for a specific problem.

The staff has helped businesses find new outlets for their products; prepare advertising copy; plan more efficient production; anticipate economic developments; map out sales territories; work out personnel policies; settle tax controversies and estates; furnish documentary evidence in law suits; prepare speeches and papers on business subjects; in short, to furnish data upon which to base sound decisions.

Although not every American small businessman can have ready access to a major business collection like the Cleveland Public Library, the chances are that his or her local public library belongs to a regional, state, or multistate network that can provide access to extensive materials and information. The state of Illinois, for example, is organized into a voluntary library and information network called ILLINET, which includes eighteen library systems and designated reference and research libraries. Any member library may borrow material from the collection maintained by the system itself or from one of the other members of the system. If that system cannot produce the book or magazine article, the request goes on to any of the reference and research libraries in Illinois participating in interlibrary loan cooperation (including, among others, the Illinois State Library, University of Illinois Library, the Chicago Public Library, as well as the John Crerar Library for medicine, science, and technology, the University of Chicago Library, and Northwestern University Library). ILLINET has a combined collection of over twenty-four million volumes.

Public libraries indirectly help in the financing of American business by generating investments from informed readers. John Deferrari, son of an immigrant fruit peddler, presented the Boston Public Library with more than a million and a half dollars in the late 1940s in appreciation of its services. This account of an interview with Mr. Deferrari by Joseph F. Dinneen appeared in the *Boston Globe* at the time:

"You say you gave this money so that others could make money as you did. How would a man go about making two or three million dollars with only the public library for equipment?"

"By doing what I did—making use of the information available at the public library."

"Where?"

"The Statistical Room, for one place. Have you ever been to the Statistical Room? Do you know what information is on tap there?"

"No."

"Drop out there sometime and look it over. Complete your education."

"And make myself a million dollars?"

"You can."

"How?"

"Study the corporation reports like I did. Find out who's behind a business. Learn all about it, and then invest your money in the right ones."

CHAPTER 5 ********************************

Reaching Out to the Poor

When Arthur Ashe, Jr., was six years old his mother died and his father took on the responsibility of raising young Arthur and his little brother, John, alone. Mr. Ashe was a playground caretaker on the city payroll in Richmond, Virginia, and it was his daily visits to the black neighborhood's playground in Brookfield Park that gave Arthur his first exposure to the sport of tennis. By the time he was seven the boy was already wielding a tennis racquet under his father's watchful eyes.

Arthur's natural ability on the tennis court soon came to the attention of the part-time tennis instructor assigned to the segregated city playground, and as the youngster continued to develop, the instructor introduced him to Dr. Walter Johnson, a black general practitioner in Lynchburg, whose special interest was encouraging promising young tennis players of his own race. Arthur soon joined the group of young people who stayed at Dr. Johnson's home during the summer months and received personal coaching from him on his tennis court.

By the time Arthur Ashe, Jr., was fourteen, he had entered his first major tennis competition, the junior national championships. He managed to reach the semifinals.

Two years later he won the junior indoor singles title, and by 1968, Arthur had become the best-known black tennis player in

U.S. history, winning both the U.S. Amateur and U.S. Open Championship titles. In 1975, he won the Wimbledon crown.

Looking back on his childhood in February 1977, Arthur Ashe, Jr., wrote "An Open Letter to Black Parents" in the sports section of *The New York Times*. It was entitled "Send Your Children to the Libraries." Mr. Ashe's thesis was simple—young blacks spend too much time on the playing field and too little time in the libraries.

> While we are 60 percent of the National Basketball Association, we are less than 4 percent of the doctors and lawyers. While we are about 35 percent of major league baseball we are less than 2 percent of the engineers. While we are about 40 percent of the National Football League, we are less than 11 percent of construction workers such as carpenters and bricklayers.

Mr. Ashe said that he often addressed high school audiences and that his message was always the same: "For every hour you spend on the athletic field, spend two in the library."

Learning has always been the key to equal opportunity in America, and the one place that is open to *all* regardless of income, educational attainment, or level of preparedness is the public library. In urging blacks to make greater use of libraries, Mr. Ashe was not speaking to black parents as an idealist but as a hardheaded pragmatist. He spoke about jobs, income levels, getting ahead, and unemployment. And he related all these to use or disuse of libraries.

> We have been on the same roads—sports and entertainment—too long. We need to pull over, fill up at the library and speed away to Congress and the Supreme Court, the unions and the business world.

Arthur Ashe was not the first member of a minority group to discover that one of the keys to equal opportunity is to be found at the public library.

Over the years many thousands of youngsters from low-income backgrounds have gained a foothold in the larger world through their community's public libraries, largely on their own. Author James Baldwin, whose books were to help ignite the civil-rights movement in the 1950s and 1960s, read his way out of Harlem at his local branch of the New York Public Library. Dr. Kenneth B. Clark, the noted educator whose study on the effects of racial discrimination provided the factual basis for the U.S. Supreme Court's landmark decision of 1954, came under the influence of the great book collector and librarian Arthur Schomburg, as a small boy growing up in Harlem. Congressman Henry B. Gonzales, growing up in San Antonio, Texas, found the library a magic carpet:

> In the public library I found a whole world of ideas. There were newspapers and magazines from everywhere, and all I had to do was go to the reading room to use them. The library stacks gave me access to all the power and magic of literature; I would spend endless hours copying poems and essays from the library. English was a new language to me, and I found that I could master ideas best by reading them again and again; and by copying long excerpts, I could have my own library.

> It was in the public library that I learned the full power of words, the endless value of ideas and knowledge stored in books —and all merely for the asking.

The problem is that traditional library services tend to reach only the better educated and more stable members of low-income communities. For all practical purposes, these services are largely unavailable to the great majority of residents of underprivileged areas.

Libraries have found that if they are to reach the disadvantaged members of their communities, they must use their resources in innovative ways. Even when a library is just down the block, many people do not know it is there, or that they are entitled to use it. Language barriers, cultural barriers, low-reading levels, and simple mistrust prevent many poverty-area people from recognizing the library as a resource capable of boosting them up to jobs and a better life.

WHO ARE THE DISADVANTAGED?

Although the term is often used, there is no accepted general definition of the word "disadvantaged." The most common factors used in identifying the disadvantaged are economic levels and education. Groups that suffer more deprivations in terms of education and economic resources than the rest of society include the poor, the elderly, the undereducated, the unemployed, and those who are treated as racial outcasts such as the American Indian, blacks, Puerto Ricans, Mexican-Americans, and Eskimos. The Appalachian Adult Education Center at Morehead, Kentucky, a group which has worked intensively with underprivileged people for many years, uses this definition: anyone over sixteen years of age who is out of school with less than a high school diploma and/or has a family income below the federal government's poverty index.

The Poor

In 1975 there were 25.9 million Americans—12 per cent of the population—living below the subsistence income poverty level as determined by the U.S. Bureau of the Census. The majority of these poor are either black, of Spanish origin, elderly, or in families headed by women. Those below the poverty level in 1974 (the most recent available figures) accounted for 10 per cent of the white population, 31 per cent of the black population, and 27 per cent of the Spanish-origin population. Most of the poor lived in metropolitan areas and 36 per cent were inner-city residents.

The Illiterate and Functionally Incompetent

A 1975 study of adult functional competency conducted for the U.S. Office of Education by the University of Texas revealed that more than twenty-three million adult Americans—one in five—lack even the rudimentary skills to cope in our society. They are unable to fill out job applications, write checks, address envelopes, dial a telephone, read a bus or traffic sign, follow instructions on a paint can, calculate take-home pay, or understand help-wanted ads.

The functionally incompetent tend to be older, undereducated, unskilled, unemployed, and living in poverty—16 per cent of the white population are in this category; 44 per cent of the black population; and 56 per cent of those with Spanish surnames.

The curse of illiteracy does not simply hobble those who cannot read. It also has a substantial impact on the literate members of society. The dependency of illiterates is usually paid for out of the tax dollars of the rest of the community. Illiteracy also contributes to the feeling of frustration and resentment of those members of society who cannot find work or make ends meet. It is no accident that a profile of all inmates in federal prisons reveals that many barely function at the fifth-grade level, or that the reading level of the entire population of New Jersey's juvenile correctional facilities is at the fourth-grade level. Chief Justice Warren E. Burger summed up the relationship of illiteracy to antisocial conduct in one sentence:

> The percentage of inmates in all institutions who cannot read or write is staggering.

Special Information Needs

In 1972, Thomas A. Childers, a professor at the Drexel University Graduate School of Library Science in Philadelphia, undertook a detailed examination into the information needs of the disadvantaged adult. Study after study suggested to Childers and his associates that while most people—educated and uneducated alike—need essentially the same kind of information to survive, the disadvantaged person needs larger remedial doses in order to bring him up to "information par" with the rest of society. More than the average, Childers reports, the disadvantaged individual needs such basic information as how to obtain subsidized housing, welfare benefits, free school lunch, medical care, and so on. Closely allied to this are needs in the area of individual rights: What am I entitled to? How do I go about getting it? How do I protect myself legally? There are also needs associated with remedial adult education and day care for children. While they are hardly unique to disadvantaged Americans, says Childers, these needs pervade their lives out of all proportion.

The disadvantaged American, more than his counterpart in general society, does not know which formal channels to tap in order to solve his problems, or what specific programs exist to respond to his needs. He watches many hours of television daily, seldom reads newspapers and magazines, and never reads books. He usually does not recognize his problems as information needs, and even when he does, is not a very active information seeker. He is locked into an informal information network of friends, neighbors, and relatives that is itself deficient in the information ordinarily available to the rest of society.

Clearly there is a widespread discrepancy between what society requires of these many millions of isolated Americans and what they are able to achieve. For them there is special meaning to the biblical injunction "The truth shall make you free."

HOW CAN PUBLIC LIBRARIES HELP THE DISADVANTAGED?

Libraries have a dramatic potential for helping the disadvantaged in our society not only to survive but also to achieve a richer, fuller life. They can help by sharpening reading skills. They can help by supplying specific information. They can help by providing links with one's cultural heritage. The difficult question is: How do you make library services available to people who do not have the motivation and characteristics of conventional library users? How do you reach people who, if they think about their community library at all, view it as an alien and fearful world, a world which may perhaps be accessible to their children in school, but certainly not to them? In an attempt to plan an organized approach to reaching potential library users among the disadvantaged, the Appalachian Adult Education Center in Kentucky identified four special groups who can be helped through library services. Their classifications reflect seven years of intensive research and work with underprivileged adults in the Appalachian states.

Group one includes "those individuals who are economically and personally secure and believe there is a beneficial return from involvement in education, library and other services." Members of this group are relatively easy to reach and serve and tend to be registered library borrowers on their own initiative.

Group two, also relatively easy to reach and serve, includes those who have suffered some disadvantage from undereducation such as continuous underemployment or inability to help their children with their homework. These people often achieve dramatic changes in economic level and life-style as a result of education and library services. The chief requirement for serving this group is a schedule of library hours to accommodate the users' long working hours.

Group three includes those who are deficient in the reading and computation skills needed for high school equivalency and a decent wage. If they are employed, it is in low-paying, dead-end, and short-term jobs. If libraries are to become available to members of this group, they need one-to-one recruitment and one-to-one services.

Group four is smallest in size but greatest in need. The AAEC calls the people in it "the stationary poor." They are unemployed, unemployable, and do not believe they have any control over their own futures. The only way they can be served by libraries is in their own homes on an individual basis.

Innovative library services have been developed in various communities to fill the needs of the disadvantaged. These services have had three major thrusts, each dependent upon the other for maximum effectiveness:

1. Reaching out into the community with services and materials carefully geared to the needs of the residents. This means gathering information about the community and developing working relationships with community organizations.

2. Establishing information and referral services that answer questions ranging from "Where can I get a VD test?" to "My daughter has been acting strange lately, what can I do?" to "Where can I go to play chess?"

3. Programs to help people learn to read.

OUTREACH PROGRAMS

"I would walk the streets ringing a bell for story hours and stop wherever there was a group of children in a place to sit. Then I would tell them where I worked. 'You know where the library is?' I would say, and they would say, 'Is that what that is?' "

That is how Willye Dennis recalls her first efforts in the 1960s to take her library into the streets of Eastside, Jacksonville, Florida, a neighborhood with a high percentage of families earning incomes below the poverty line, a high percentage of adults with a less than eighth-grade education, high unemployment, and poor housing standards. Many of the children came from homes void of books, periodicals, or newspapers. Many saw little of their parents and therefore missed what stimulation of verbal skills they might have obtained from them. Mrs. Dennis' street stories satisfied a great hunger for learning.

Today Mrs. Dennis sees to it that thousands of underprivileged children listen to stories. As supervisor of Jacksonville's outreach program for the last seven years, she has been sending two mini-bookmobiles five days a week to regularly scheduled stops at Eastside Headstart centers, day-care centers, playgrounds, and low-income apartment complexes. The bookmobiles are stocked with storytellers, psychedelic flannel boards, dulcimers, autoharps, and bongo drums ("can't tell an African folk story without a bongo background"), paperback editions of *Curious George, Clifford, The Big Red Dog, Richard Scarry's ABC Word Book,* and many more titles that any child may borrow and take home. No library cards are required. Explains Mrs. Dennis, "We are attempting to attest to the fact that learning can be fun."

Outreach is not a new phenomenon. In the early 1940s, a young librarian named Margaret Edwards, working for Enoch Pratt Free Library in Baltimore, rented a vegetable peddler's horse and wagon, filled the wagon with shelving, the shelving with books, and peddled reading in the slums. The horse wore a funny hat and Margaret would play on a xylophone to let people know she was there. Kids would swarm around her begging to drive the horse or "beat the pianner." While their mothers looked over the selections, the youngsters would crawl up on the wagon and sing from songbooks. Each day the wagon circulated about the same number of books as the neighborhood branch. Over the years, outreach programs have taken many forms.

Taking the Library Out on the Road

Today bookmobiles flash across the New Mexico desert to Navajo Reservation outposts. They crawl up narrow Appalachian hollows to isolated communities. In California, a Biblioteca Ambulante brings films in both English and Spanish, as well as records, paperbacks, comic books, and books purchased in Mexico, to large numbers of farmworkers and migrants in the outlying parts of four central counties. The potential of the bookmobile is being realized in urban and rural settings alike. The key ingredients are simply money and imagination.

Locating Libraries Where the People Are

Part of the effort to take the library to the people has been the opening of new branches where neighborhood people naturally congregate. Storefront libraries have sprung up on major shopping streets in ghetto neighborhoods. In Tulsa, Oklahoma, and Houston, Texas, residents can find new branch libraries handily located next to their community health centers or service centers housing the facilities of such organizations as Planned Parenthood and Legal Aid. The new community building on the Winnebago Indian Reservation in northeast Nebraska houses the Leonia Johnson Memorial Public Library, along with the tribal council offices, Headstart headquarters, and the offices of senior citizen and young adult groups.

Not long ago a branch librarian in Memphis, Tennessee, walked into a place in her community where food stamps were being given out and noticed the huge crowds of people waiting for their stamps, most of them mothers with young children in tow. The waiting area is now a small library. Those waiting in line can leaf through issues of *Ebony* and *Jet,* borrow paperback copies of *Black Like Me, Roots,* or biographies of black leaders; find out about the adult basic education classes given at the local library, and four days a week the children waiting with their mothers can listen to story hours given by the librarian.

Neighborhood librarians are discovering new ways of linking up with members of the community who never knew that their public library was anything more than a place for kids to do homework.

Workshop sessions for neighborhood residents help librarians learn what to provide in terms of services and materials. For example, at Baltimore's Hollins-Payson Branch in the heart of Baltimore's inner city, adult basic education classes for people at less than an eighth-grade reading level started up recently as a direct result of a community workshop that brought together residents and people from different service agencies to talk about what they would like to see the library do.

Community Walks

"Community walks" are becoming a valuable part of branch library outreach efforts in some urban areas. A Detroit librarian describes how their community walk program works:

> We walked from our branch libraries to the neighborhood grocery, barber shop, police station, variety store, pharmacy, gas station, and wherever else we could find. We told people, our own public, that the library can help them, that the library on the corner two blocks away can answer questions, not just questions about books, school, and homework, but questions about their lives, their problems, and their own community.
>
> The response was, in every sense, overwhelming. On the spot, people asked for a notary public, a part-time employee, someone to call about a cracked and broken sidewalk, and where and how to apply for Social Security benefits. They asked, our public, if the library would lend space for a block club meeting, if the library would like to join the neighborhood business associations, if the library would attend the next police community relations meeting. They presented us, in very clear and concise terms, with their informational needs and then they asked us to respond to those needs.

Through community walks librarians are acquiring a new depth of knowledge about the members of the neighborhoods they serve. Robert Croneberger, a librarian who has been a leader in developing outreach techniques, tells the story of the Detroit Public Library's repeated efforts a few years back to reach out to a recent influx of Iraqis. The library, where he was employed at the time as deputy director, distributed flyers and posters printed in Arabic, but with no results. Then the librarians went out into the community and learned their new neighbors were Chaldeans, Catholic Iraqis with a distinctive language, religion, and culture different from that of their Arab Iraqi oppressors from whom they had fled. Arabic was most decidedly *not* the language with which to attract them to the library. Instead, the library was able to contact the recent immigrants through a multiethnic community organization that had a sizable and active representation from the hard-to-reach Chaldeans. Not long after that initiative was taken, members of the group began to find their way to the library to seek information about their new home and new life.

Breaking down Communication Barriers

Librarians are increasingly overcoming the cultural and language barriers that prevent members of minority groups from using the library services to which they are entitled. In New York City's South Bronx where two hundred thousand Puerto Rican and other Spanish-speaking people are concentrated, the key to effective service has been the use of a community liaison assistant, a Spanish-speaking nonlibrarian who serves as a strong connecting link between the neighborhood and each of the nine branch libraries serving the area. The South Bronx is synonymous in the minds of many New Yorkers with the most degrading living conditions in the city—blocks of vacant, burned-out buildings; many of the occupied buildings without running water; 40 per cent of the residents on welfare; 30 per cent of the employable unemployed. The community liaison assistant works directly with schools, churches, poverty agencies, community centers, and political and social clubs. In this way the community is informed about free library services, books, and materials and is encouraged to come into the library. Each branch library has a Spanish-speaking staff member to help the individual library user in either Spanish or English. Materials in both Spanish and English concentrate on practical needs, including vocational and adult education. Emphasis on the historical and cultural heritage of the Spanish-speaking people is strong. When people started coming into the libraries in the South Bronx in response to this program, the majority of their inquiries had to do with survival:

"Can you help me write a letter for food stamps for my grandmother and me?"

"My little girl, she can't read 'cause she doesn't see too good. Do you have glasses?"

"Somebody said you know about civil service jobs."

At other places across the nation, low levels of literacy and the lack of printed materials in native languages present obstacles for librarians in reaching another American minority group, our Indian population. In New Mexico, for example, the Indians' first language is their own, in many different dialects; Spanish is often the second language; and English is the third. Indians living in cities—nearly half the total American Indian population—tend to become lost in the general population and are therefore particularly difficult to reach. In Sioux City (Iowa), St. Paul (Minnesota), Chicago, and Cleveland, the public libraries work with American Indian centers, usually through an Indian library staff member, to plan literacy and cultural programs, to supply portable libraries of paperbacks, as well as information and referral services. In some instances programs started by libraries are now being run entirely by American Indian centers.

Hundreds of thousands of immigrants from non-English-speaking and non-Western cultures have come to the United States since revision of the U.S. immigration law in 1964. Public libraries are helping these people adjust to American life, just as they helped earlier generations of new Americans.

Mountain View, California, is a small city thirty-five miles south of San Francisco that has experienced a recent influx of Vietnamese, Cambodians, Laotians, Filipinos, and people from the Portuguese Azores. Here the local public library works closely with the local adult education department. In addition to providing a reading laboratory and a full-scale program of tutoring in English, adult education teachers bring their classes in for tours. "These often last several hours," explains Brenda Gray, the librarian in charge. "Usually students bring in a whole sheet of questions and we go through the entire routine of how to find materials." To encourage library use by those who are just beginning to learn English, the librarians stress that the library is not limited to books; there are art prints, language records and cassettes, even dressmaking patterns that require no knowledge of English to be taken out and enjoyed. Mountain View Public Library also has special language collections, and the librarians show the students how to find materials in their native tongues. Students usually receive a library card and start taking out materials on their first visit. The library has also set up a substantial circulating collection of beginning adult reading material as part of its commitment to help the recent immigrants at each stage of their developing mastery of the English language.

INFORMATION AND REFERRAL SERVICES

Banner posters plastered on the sides of public buses in the city of Memphis ask in bright red letters against a yellow background: "NEED HELP? NEED INFORMATION? CALL *LINC,* 528-2999." The number is that of the Memphis Public Library's Information Center.

In Detroit, the number to call is 833-4000, or any one of the Detroit Public Library's twenty-six branches. Information and referral services are fairly new to the public-library landscape, but they are rapidly becoming a standard service in every region of the United States—from Montclair, New Jersey, to Wake County, North Carolina, to Chicago (where Spanish-speaking librarians answer calls on a special line); to Houston, Texas. Their purpose: to link up an individual with the service, activity, information, or advice that fits his need.

The Detroit TIP program (The Information Place), which began in 1972, is the first and one of the best information and referral centers. TIP keeps track of some fifteen hundred organizations—any type that provides some kind of service to the public from health, education, and welfare services to chess clubs and cooking classes. For each agency there are perhaps ten separate headings directing the inquirer to that service, thereby providing roughly fifteen thousand information entries to needed services. Information is constantly updated, both at the central library and at the branches. The program receives from five thousand to eight thousand telephone requests a month, plus a couple of thousand in-person queries from people who come to the library itself. The TIP service is available seven days a week.

TIP can tell inquirers where to get a senior citizen bus card, where to get a cancer checkup, where to learn a trade. People calling for information about nursing homes can be put in touch with an organization called Citizens for Better Care, a group familiar with nursing home care in the area; people with landlord-tenant problems may be referred to the Small Claims Court or a legal aid service that will help them specifically with a landlord-tenant dispute. A low-income mother who worries there is something wrong with her child's diet, or who calls because she has heard about "some place" where she can get special food for her baby is directed to a supplemental food program run by the Detroit Department of Health for pregnant or breast-feeding women and for children under four years of age. TIP gets a lot of phone calls from people who want to go back to secondary school but don't know how to go about it. They are told where they may go for preparatory classes for a high school equivalency examination.

TIP librarians take time to give inquirers enough information so that they can deal with the situation for themselves. TIP also follows up on many of its referrals. A man in need of medical care who had been refused service by his doctor when he discovered that his patient was no longer covered by medical insurance recently called TIP for help. The librarian referred the caller to Detroit General Hospital for free medical treatment and smoothed the way at the clinic by calling and making an appointment for him. The caller was upset at having to take "charity" for the first time in his life. The librarian explained to him that as a taxpayer he was entitled to free medical service. The librarian took the man's name and phone number and later followed up to see how the hospital referral worked out.

A black woman on public assistance with four children called TIP in utter frustration. She needed to go into the hospital for an operation, but because she had no proof that she was covered by Medicaid, the hospital would not admit her. Although she was indeed covered, her social worker, harried and overworked, was not taking steps to help her. Phone calls by the librarian to the community affairs office of the Michigan Department of Social Services and to the hospital straightened out the matter. It was simply a question of someone interceding for the woman and verbalizing her need. A librarian filled the bill.

By indexing their community's social and recreational services, the public library gains a unique overview of community facilities. This has also allowed the library in some instances to help bring about needed change.

In Memphis, for example, it became evident to the referral-service librarians that there existed no free burial service of any kind for city residents, not even a potter's field, and that this worked considerable hardship for poor families. Through neighborhood contacts which the branch librarians had already established in the course of their "community walks," the librarians were able to make arrangements with funeral directors in the disadvantaged areas for free funeral services and burial plots in cases referred to them by social workers from the Memphis Department of Human Services.

Also in Memphis, a program suggested by the library's information and referral service has helped to coordinate the giving of Christmas toys and food baskets to poor families by church and social groups.

Ironically, such information services in public libraries have proved so effective that as many as 50 per cent of the inquiries come from public agencies seeking information about services provided by *other* agencies—an unanticipated result which dramatizes the void that exists in centralized information sources.

A variety of techniques must be utilized to uncover a full knowledge of community resources. Through churches, Lions clubs, the Black Knights of Mallory, and even bars and barbershops, many public libraries have become part of an informal community network. In one case, the only effective way a public library could provide information and referral services to a strongly religious Eastern European neighborhood was for the librarians to arrange for neighborhood priests to act as intermediaries. The priests called the library for the necessary information which they then relayed to their parishioners.

Although the prime target of these new community information and referral services is the disadvantaged, the services do not stop there. Many people from all income levels make use of these public-library services to help them grapple with the complex problems which face all citizens in an increasingly regulated society.

LITERACY PROGRAMS

A forty-year-old unemployed factory worker, who dropped out of school in third grade, walks into the Enoch Pratt central library in Baltimore. He is there, he tells the librarian, because he believes that by learning to read better he will be able to get a job. She enrolls him in a program to receive individual tutoring from one of seventeen specially trained literacy tutors working in Baltimore's public-library system. At his first lesson, the pupil is asked by his tutor about some recent experience, perhaps to describe what he did that day. The tutor writes down his words as he says them and these words become the basis for his first reading lesson. The only requirement for receiving instruction: the desire to learn.

For two hours each week at the Brooklyn Public Library, more than thirty pairs of tutors and students settle in at the big wooden tables in the Art and Music wing, their flash cards, workbooks, and yellow legal pads spread in front of them. Sessions are tailored to student needs and include how to tell time, fill out job applications, and read information on packages they buy in the supermarket.

At the Jacob Edwards Memorial Library in Southbridge, Massachusetts, some forty tutors work with foreign-born adults who want to learn to speak, read, and write English.

These teams are part of the tremendous upswing in library-based literacy tutoring, a development spurred by the discovery that millions of Americans—about one in five—cannot read. In fact, less than half the American adult population is considered proficient at reading. The adult basic education program of the U.S. Office of Education—once regarded as the major effort to reduce adult illiteracy—has reached only a small fraction of those in need of literacy training, according to a recent report to the Congress by the comptroller general.

The basic education program works with groups of adults in classes. The one-to-one tutoring used in the library programs is generally recognized as a more effective technique, particularly among the most deficient readers.

Why should libraries take on the responsibility of tutoring in reading? Libraries have the space, they have the materials, and, as Robert Wedgeworth, executive director of the American Library Association, explains it: "When people come into the library to look at help-wanted ads in the paper and can barely understand what's written, then it's time for the librarian to step in where other American educational institutions have failed." Tutors have found that the bookish but relaxed, undemanding atmosphere of the library is particularly helpful in dispelling many of the anxieties of adult learners. For someone who cannot read, the simple act of entering a library, a place heretofore out of bounds to him or her, can bring a real psychological boost.

The use of volunteers in one-to-one tutoring makes financially possible a program that would otherwise be prohibitively expensive. Many of the tutors teaching basic literacy skills—whether they be library staff members or volunteers from the community—have been trained by the Literacy Volunteers of America, a growing nonprofit organization started thirteen years ago in Syracuse, New York. In other cities such as Memphis and Philadelphia, libraries work with Laubach Literacy, Incorporated, a group which implements a teaching technique known the world over as the "each one teach one" method. It was started in the 1920s by the missionary Dr. Frank Laubach during his years among the Moro people of the Philippines. Both of these groups train volunteers to work with individuals whose skills range from zero literacy to about a fifth-grade reading level. Students are then encouraged to go on to become volunteer tutors themselves.

The approach to library-based tutoring varies from community to community. The public library in Tulsa, Oklahoma, arranged for two of their librarians to receive training in teaching illiterates and they in turn have been training additional staff. Many libraries simply coordinate and sponsor reading programs—giving space, helping to secure teachers, providing publicity and promotion for the programs, and, most important, supplying the needed materials for both students and teachers. Numerous public libraries also provide space and materials for adult basic education classes as well as preparatory classes for high school equivalency examinations.

Federal funds under the 1974 Right to Read Act (a multifaceted program intended to stimulate innovative reading programs) have enabled a few libraries to reach larger numbers of people. The Denver Public Library is currently tutoring on a one-to-one basis some four hundred students with less than sixth-grade competency. Students and tutors work wherever it is convenient— in the library's learning center situated in the heavily Chicano area of Denver's southwest side, in churches, in community centers, and in people's homes.

Ironically, one of the serious problems in literacy programs for adults is finding good reading material. The tutors emphasize that success depends directly on how relevant and interesting the reading materials are to the individual student. Literature designed to teach children to read ("See Spot run. Run, Spot, run.") is seldom suitable for adults, whose experience as parents, employees, and as members of a community give them an entirely different range of experiences and interests. One study found that subjects of particular interest to adult illiterates included Langston Hughes's poetry, hints on careful buying, information about better jobs, selected readings from the Bible, biographical sketches, and topics of sociological interest. Julia Palmer, a volunteer who organized a bookmobile project in a low-income section of Brooklyn ten years ago, recently published a list of titles which proved popular with young and old readers ("Read for Your Life"), and has now organized the American Reading Council to stimulate wider interest in library services for the poor.

The librarians in the Reader Development Program at the Free Library of Philadelphia have become experts in identifying and evaluating hard-to-find materials for adults written at or below the eighth-grade reading skill level. Their annotated reading lists of special materials are invaluable resources for other libraries and organizations concerned with combating illiteracy. The Philadelphia program has been in operation since 1967 and supplies paperback books, pamphlets, filmstrips, and recordings to a wide range of agencies throughout the city. Users include prisons, church literacy programs, Board of Education adult basic education classes, and specialized agencies such as the Philadelphia Adult Basic Education Academy, a private, nonprofit organization that tutors some two hundred fifty people a year who begin with zero literacy.

✓ Some of the innovative materials the Free Library of Philadelphia makes available for these learners include workbooks which provide practice in filling out application forms; a math book that uses paychecks, shopping, home improvement loans, and automobile insurance as the means for bringing the subject alive; and a series of carefully abridged versions of well-known books of fiction such as *Dracula* and *A Tree Grows in Brooklyn,* plus autobiographies of Frederick Douglass, Althea Gibson, and Gordon Parks.

Critical to further literacy development for someone who has acquired partial literacy skill is easy access to appropriate reading materials. Many public libraries make available books and pamphlets specially designed to encourage new adult readers to exercise their skills. "Life-coping" pamphlets, written in a style and vocabulary aimed at adults who read at fifth- to seventh-grade levels, can be found in all forty-seven branches of the Free Library of Philadelphia. The pamphlets deal with such practical problems as how to make use of employment, health, and other service agencies; how to recognize symptoms of illness; how to take out citizenship papers; how to get a driver's license; and how to resolve a landlord-tenant dispute. One two-volume pamphlet describes fifty different job fields and occupations and tells the adult reader how to obtain more information. Another series includes such titles as "Be Informed on Money," "Be Informed on Marriage," "Be Informed on Banking," "Be Informed on Nutrition."

The gratifications for volunteers who invest their time in helping adults overcome illiteracy can be immense. Not long ago, Barbara Caturani of the Queens Borough (New York) Public Library, saw one of her alumni, Edward Moses, a young black man with enormous educational handicaps but a strong desire to overcome them, promoted to store manager for a large retail chain after he had mastered the ability to read and write. When she presented him to a meeting of Literacy Volunteers, the audience listened in hushed silence as he recited the following piece of poetry he had composed with the aid of his newfound skills:

"I would like to write a poem.
That's right, a poem.
A poem that enters the heart and soul of all people.
A poem that expresses the light of understanding
And tells of the rhythm within the wisdom.
The kind that beats to the melody of life.
One that tells of the rich and poor and more.
A poem that is filled with enjoyment and love for all.
One to tell of the good and bad times of my life, of my mind.
And of the times when you feel
The deep, dark Shadow of the Night enclose your body.
A poem to replenish the cold, lonely spot of your inner soul
With precious dreams and beautiful memories.
To tell all I want to tell you, it will take more than a poem.
I promise to tell you everything with the poem that is my life."

COMMUNITY INVOLVEMENT

The vitality that can come to library service in disadvantaged areas is exemplified by the Queens Borough (New York) Public Library's Langston Hughes Community Library and Cultural Center, a community-controlled and community-staffed storefront library located in a low-income, largely black neighborhood. Known as Corona-East Elmhurst, the community where the library is now located is populated by thirty thousand people. By the late 1960s, it was deteriorating into a hard-core disadvantaged area. The community's leaders decided to do something about it, and one of the things they decided was that they needed a library. During the first week of library operation in 1969 more than fifteen hundred residents visited the remodeled storefront, almost one thousand adult books were taken out, and over four hundred library cards were issued.

A Library Action Committee composed entirely of members of the community is responsible for hiring the supervisor of the Langston Hughes Center, establishing policy, and operating the library center in conjunction with the Queens Borough Public Library. The people who staff the library are all residents of the immediate area.

Corona-East Elmhurst was a neighborhood of people totally unfamiliar with libraries, card catalogues, and call slips. For the first seven years at Langston Hughes, the book collections—largely paperback—were not catalogued. Multiple copies were arranged in simple reader-interest classification. A color-code system identified subject areas—green for fiction, gold for biographies, red for general reading, and so on. There were no fines for overdues. People returned books when they were finished with them. Now the Dewey decimal system is being incorporated along with the existing color-code system so that patrons may become familiar with the traditional procedures they can expect to encounter in other libraries.

People are encouraged to turn to the Langston Hughes Community Library for answers to their questions. The library maintains an up-to-date information and referral file with emphasis on survival information; it has video and slide tapes dealing with such subjects as how to go about getting food stamps and how to apply for public assistance. The library is also used as a center for meetings of PTA groups, the Welfare Rights Mothers' organization, the Consumer Education Board of Corona-East Elmhurst, and numerous other community groups.

There are workshops in art, poetry, African textile design, photography, creative writing, and more. There is a theatre arts workshop for children eight to twelve years of age. There is a homework assistance program for elementary and high school students every weekday afternoon. There is an exercise class for mothers whose preschool youngsters are enjoying a story hour in the library. On Saturdays black schoolteachers from the neighborhood, members of the Delta Sigma Beta sorority, tutor students in grades three to six who need remedial work in mathematics and reading.

Performers who have appeared at the Langston Hughes Community Library have included poets, karate groups, jazz quartets,

African dancers and drummers, a black master of magic, the publisher of *Black Sports,* and the Community Children's Drama Group.

Community interest in the Langston Hughes Library and Cultural Center has remained high. In late 1972 when a 50 per cent cutback in federal funds would have forced a reduction in staff from twenty to only four members, community residents packed a fund-raising dance in sufficient numbers to allow the full staff to remain on salary until the city administration came through with additional funds two months later. The city was encouraged to take this action by the demonstration of political and community support for the center at an evening political caucus and an afternoon motorcade through the neighborhood.

In recent years the community around Langston Hughes Library has been upgraded. Buildings are being renovated; new businesses are starting up. The Walter White Manpower Center has opened across the street and a drug rehabilitation facility is nearby. With the library as a focal point of interest and activity, the neighborhood is no longer on the decline.

GIVING MEANING TO EQUAL OPPORTUNITY

More than two hundred years have passed since Thomas Jefferson and his colleagues at Philadelphia asserted as a self-evident truth that "All men are created equal." Ironically, our computer-based, highly industrialized society, and increasingly benevolent government have made equality harder to achieve for many citizens than it was for most in the simpler setting of the eighteenth century. To realize "equal opportunity" in present-day America, one needs to be able to find where the opportunities are and be able to utilize them. This often demands more knowledge, skills, and sophistication than some of the most educated citizens possessed two centuries ago.

Increasing numbers of Americans have fallen behind the higher levels of education and skills needed to gain employment and to manage and care for a family. America today faces the distressing reality of greater inequality, rather than less, for hundreds of thousands of its citizens.

A number of government and private programs have attempted to bridge the gap between the "advantaged" and "disadvantaged." Few have succeeded. The result is that countless Americans live in worlds of ignorance and poverty.

Public libraries do not possess any panacea for this paradox, but they do provide some powerful weapons for dealing with it. With their decentralized network of branches to serve local communities, with librarians professionally trained in the skills of organizing and maintaining reference materials, and with already established collections of backup reference materials, libraries are the logical community agencies to provide across-the-board information and referral services as well as support for literacy programs.

In addition, the public library is probably the least threatening of institutions to the insecure person with limited education; no one has anything to lose by asking at the library. As the slogan for one library puts it, "You don't have to read to use the library, just pick up the phone and call us." Or just come on in.

The thousands of public libraries across the nation are the logical resources to bring to the task of correcting inequality. As they have for newly arrived immigrants from foreign shores for many generations, public libraries can supply needed information, literacy, guidance, and self-assurance to those who are at the bottom end of the economic and educational ladder. Innovative librarians and creative community leaders have already shown the way. The challenge for the rest of us is to fashion a lasting program.

CHAPTER 6

Protecting Our Rights and Liberties

Historians looking back at the mid-twentieth century will easily single out one individual as the horseman who awakened the nation to the threat to our environment caused by mindless politics of government and industry. That person was a small, quiet woman who wielded a powerful pen—Rachel Carson. Her best-selling book, *Silent Spring,* jolted complacent officials who had accepted DDT and other pesticides as "progress," into a realization that they were poisoning the earth and inflicting irreversible damage.

> We stand now where two roads diverge [she wrote]. But unlike the roads in Robert Frost's familiar poem, they are not equally fair. The road we have long been traveling is deceptively easy, a smooth superhighway on which we progress at great speed, but at its end lies disaster. The other fork of the road—the one "less traveled by"—offers our last, our only chance to reach a destination that assures the preservation of our earth.

Powerful leaders heeded her warnings, in addition to hundreds of thousands of concerned citizens. Supreme Court Justice William O. Douglas called her book "the most important chronicle of this century for the human race." *Silent Spring* received a string of awards and unstinting praise from the media. Typical was the appraisal of it in *Saturday Review,* which described the work as "a devastating attack on human carelessness, greed and irresponsibility."

It should be read by every American who does not want it to be the epitaph of a world not very far beyond us in time.

Rachel Carson did not live to see the changes her writing brought about. But those who responded to her alarms were quick to recognize the leadership she had given. When President Lyndon B. Johnson signed one of the first pieces of legislation to bring pesticide use under control he went out of his way to recognize her role.

She would have been proud of this bill and of this moment. We owe much to her and to those who still work for the cause of a safer and healthier America.

Silent Spring is an "issue" book. It ranks with Jacob Riis's *How the Other Half Lives,* Lincoln Steffens' *The Shame of Cities,* and other notable issue books, which have had profound impact on public attitudes and government policies. It is part of a larger group of literally hundreds of issue books which have contributed in greater or lesser degree to the shaping of our destiny as a people and a nation, books like Michael Harrington's *The Other America* and Ralph Nader's *Unsafe at Any Speed.* All of these issue books have one thing in common: They are written by *individuals.* Not by the news media or official agencies or "the establishment." They are the work product of people with ideas and commitment who have found a vehicle of expression that can influence their fellow citizens and their elected representatives. These are society's dissenters who change the course of our history in varying degrees; true exponents of free speech and free press. Issue books are basic to the preservation of our freedoms.

Issue books are created out of tough-minded reporting and endless, dogged library research. Rachel Carson was explicit in her acknowledgment of library research in the writing of *Silent Spring:*

Every writer of a book on many diverse facts owes much to the skill and helpfulness of librarians.

The nature of Miss Carson's work required the use of technical research and reference libraries. She utilized three assistants to help her with the "enormous task of library research." A mute testimonial to the magnitude of that research was the book's listing of published source materials, which was fifty-five pages long.

Libraries not only provide research materials for issue books, but these libraries in turn become repositories for new issue books, both to serve citizen readers and also future researchers and writers of tomorrow's issue books.

Unlike the gothic novel and other sure money-makers, the issue book can be a risky investment for book publishers. Often the factor that makes the difference in a decision to publish is the prospect of sales to libraries. Library book sales represent a half-billion dollars per year, and without them as many as half of the new titles published each year would not be economically possible. A recent *Publishers Weekly* survey disclosed that for almost 25 per cent of the nation's nontextbook publishers, library sales account for the major share of revenues. Half of such publishers count on at least 40 per cent of their sales going to the library market.

Without libraries, most issue books would not be written, published, or placed in circulation.

PUBLIC LIBRARIES AND THE NEWS MEDIA

Newspapers are the lifeblood of democracy. Dailies numbering 1,775 and weeklies totaling 7,650 keep the nation on its toes. They inform their readers of vital issues, expose fraud and misconduct in government, provide a ready voice of dissent. Millions of Americans in every walk of life depend on them every day.

What good people never stop to realize is that newspapers in turn depend on public libraries as a basic source of information to pass on to their readers. Current news, of course, usually comes directly from events and human sources. But behind many stories lie important background facts which are provided by public libraries. In some fields, especially those involving local history, public libraries actually play a dominant role as the source for newspaper stories.

To determine exactly what use newspapers make of public libraries, the research staff of the National Citizens Emergency Committee to Save Our Public Libraries recently directed inquiries to a sampling of journalists across the country. The majority said that they used public libraries as a prime backup for their information resources, even though many newspapers have their own internal libraries. The following comments tell the story effectively:

CALIFORNIA—*San Francisco Chronicle,* Suzanne Caster, head librarian:

Undoubtedly, the San Francisco Public Library, along with other such libraries in our area, is one of our most indispensable sources of information outside of our own organization.

Often, by telephone, we seek out factual material that supplements that which is not complete here in our clippings or reference works. In a deadline situation this can be an invaluable service.

Reporters and writers often visit individual libraries to continue long-term research and to borrow books for use in preparation of interviews, feature articles, and/or news stories. These materials include all areas of fiction and nonfiction. Upon occasion our news desks and copy desks borrow materials that can be reproduced for illustrating stories.

FLORIDA—*St. Petersburg Times,* Eugene Patterson, editor:

The public library is the place a newspaperman goes when a story is too important to be scratched together from old clippings and a drawer full of notes. It's the most important bank in anybody's town.

ILLINOIS—*Chicago Daily News,* Daryle M. Feldmeir, editor:

It would be impossible for me to document the number of times the Chicago Public Library has proved to be a special ally of a *Daily News* reporter in search of a story. I do know that without the public library the whole community would suffer.

LOUISIANA—*Baton Rouge Morning Advocate,* Lou Thomas, librarian:

We have found the public libraries in our city of tremendous benefit. They are used primarily by our writers, both staff and free-lance, in gathering background material for their newspaper stories. One elusive fact may require extensive research.

Our library staff confers regularly with the reference departments of the state library, which is located here, and the municipal library. A small special library such as ours cannot economically justify the kind of book collection which would be required to handle the varied questions reporters may need to have answered in the writing of a story, particularly one with in-depth treatment.

We enjoy extremely good cooperation with our public libraries and call on them for checking facts of a very current nature. Our periodical holdings are limited and many times this is the only source for reporters to use.

Because newspapers constantly strive to keep the public informed—not just in the matter of today's news, but also in the education of their readers with the "why" and "how" of matters of environment, our heritage, current legislation, recreation, and man's day-to-day needs and desires, they will continue to need the resources of public libraries to provide a meaningful service in a complex society.

PUBLIC LIBRARIES AND A FREE PRESS

Important as newspapers and broadcast media are in communicating information to the citizen, they are not the only source of material on vital issues. Of equal significance in their own right are periodicals and books—an area of the free press where the participation of public libraries is even more direct.

Ever since Thomas Paine used his pen to rally dissatisfied colonials to support the American Revolution, government leaders in this country have had a healthy respect for the pamphleteer. In modern times the pamphleteer has become the magazine writer, who often combines investigative research and pungent analysis to move his fellow citizens to action in countless fields—such as politics, consumerism, environmental protection, public health, education, welfare reform. Many of the smaller journals which focus on ideas receive little or no advertising revenues. Their existence depends on paid subscriptions, and for many of them, public libraries provide the largest single bloc of subscribers. Public-library sales keep many periodicals going, while at the same time supplying an invaluable research and reference tool to library users.

In 1975, the National Science Foundation, concerned about the economic health of scientific journals, funded a broad study of periodicals committed to independent thought and research by Bernard Fry and Herbert S. White, both of whom are with Indiana University's Graduate Library School. Their study examined the economic interface between publishers of scholarly and research journals and the public, academic, and special libraries expected to purchase these journals. The survey showed rapid deterioration in financial viability of university presses in the study period, 1969–73. "The situation for university presses," they reported, "can be described, without exaggeration, as disastrous." The researchers noted that individual subscriptions to scholarly and research journals dropped steadily for most publisher groups over the five-year period. Fewer and fewer individuals can afford the increased rates imposed by publishers faced with alarming increases in production costs. Librarians, as the largest and heretofore dependable market for subscriptions, simultaneously find themselves faced with yearly increases in journal prices, prices which consume an even greater proportion of their static and declining budgets. The research team concluded, "Despite the best efforts of publishers to hold down costs and despite the best efforts of libraries to increase acquisition budgets, the present practice is at best an uncontrollable spiral which spells extinction for a number of substantively valuable journals." Cutbacks in library purchases of periodical subscriptions because of municipal budget squeezes pose a serious threat to the basic structure by which knowledge is disseminated and to the needs of a free and democratic society.

PUBLIC LIBRARIES AND
ACCESS TO INFORMATION

Public libraries are the citizens' news "morgue." Virtually every public library has a file of back issues, at least of the local newspaper. Anyone who wants some information from a back newspaper—a student doing local history research, a government investigator checking consumer prices, a political candidate researching votes by his opponent—all turn to the public library.

Most daily newspapers refer reader inquiries for stories in back issues to the local public library. The Detroit Public Library, for example, maintains a file of back issues of the *Detroit Free Press* on microfilm, and all inquiries made to the newspaper are automatically routed to the library.

Many libraries have more than local newspapers available. Over eight hundred libraries across the country subscribe to the *New York Times Index* and also to the special service which supplies all back issues of the *Times* on microfilm.

For his monumental work, *The Brooklyn Bridge,* David McCullough sought out back copies of more than thirty different newspapers, ranging from the *Boston Post* to the *Troy Record,* in more than fifteen separate libraries to tell the story "of the most famous bridge in the world and . . . the context of the age from which it sprang."

Barbara Tuchman tells of her astonishment and delight, when she was researching her book, *Stilwell and the American Experience,* at finding in the New York Public Library "a full run of *The Sentinel,* the weekly journal of the 15th Infantry, stationed in Tientsin, to which Stilwell was attached in the crucial years 1926–29 when Chiang Kai-Shek reached national power. In its pages," she reported, "was a series of articles, which up to then I had not known existed, by Major Stilwell, my protagonist, on the personalities and issues and climactic events of that time."

A French author researching the life of Stephen Crane, author of *The Red Badge of Courage,* traveled from Paris to Port Jervis, New York (Crane's hometown), to examine old issues of the *Union Gazette* in the public library there.

Some public libraries have collections of newspapers of special interest. Boston Public Library's newspaper room keeps bound files of newspapers from colonial and early American days in the Boston and New England area. The Boston library currently subscribes to 220 newspapers, 150 domestic and 70 foreign. The California State Library has a card index of two million entries in California newspapers from 1846 to date.

Current and back issues of periodicals are also major sources of information available primarily at public libraries. A member of Maine's Board of Environmental Protection, who lives along an isolated section of the Maine coast, depends on the periodicals section of the Portland (Maine) Public Library to keep up with environmental affairs. In July 1976, she reported having just read an article on Russian nuclear power plants in *The Bulletin of Atomic Scientists* supplied to her by the Portland Public Library: "In the mail this morning, [the periodicals staff] sent me a copy of an article on nuclear energy which appeared in the *Scientific American* January issue."

As a citizen activist the same person was involved with a neighborhood group that successfully opposed the improper locating of a solid waste baling station. To support their arguments, "We used articles from the magazine *The American City* and also researched the history of the baler and the Solid Waste Management Committee as it appeared in the local newspapers for the last 5 years." The newspapers were on microfilm at the library.

PUBLIC LIBRARIES AND
FEDERAL GOVERNMENT PUBLICATIONS

In the course of going about the nation's business, the three branches of the federal government generate literally tons of printed documents, a vast public record of government activity and a vital research resource on public issues. Documents range from bills before Congress, public laws, committee reports on bills, the *Congressional Record,* and reports of government agencies covering topics in nearly the entire field of knowledge. Possibly the most important are the printed records of congressional hearings, with testimony by expert witnesses who have made exhaustive studies of a given subject and often provide the most comprehensive information extant. There are also many government publications which are virtually the *only* source of information on particular topics, such as military defense, geologic mapping, and government research projects into health, crime, safety, working conditions, and countless other areas of activities.

In recognition of the need to provide local citizen access to this great body of information, Congress in the nineteenth century established a policy of making publications about the activities of the federal government available to the general public through designated public and academic libraries. Those libraries which met certain specifications became "depository libraries" for distribution of publications issued by all branches of the federal establishment. Congressional policy as to the purpose of this program is currently set forth in Title 44, United States Code, Section 1911:

> Depository libraries shall make government publications available for the free use of the general public. . . .

THE PRESENT SYSTEM OF DEPOSITORY LIBRARIES

Through a group of 2,010 libraries—both public and academic—the Government Printing Office distributes annually more than 37,700 different document titles. In fiscal 1976, the Government Printing Office shipped a staggering 25,000,000 copies of documents to depositories. Forty-eight of these depository libraries have what is known as regional status and are therefore required to maintain collections of all government documents. The remaining libraries may be selective in their choice of documents, accepting some and declining others. Administration of the system is therefore something of a nightmare. The following is a random sampling of agencies whose reports are made available for free distribution to depository libraries:

Agricultural Marketing Service
Food and Nutrition Service
Soil Conservation Service
Civil Rights Commission
Economic Development Administration
Patent and Trademark Office
Defense Department
Environmental Protection Agency
Federal Trade Commission
Office of Education
Public Health Service
Social Security Administration

While the libraries receive these documents free of charge, they receive no assistance from the federal government in meeting the costs of storage, record keeping, preservation, and service. The concept of regional depository libraries with complete collections of government documents is excellent, but few libraries can afford these costs, certainly few public ones, the type most accessible to the general public. As a consequence, only seven states have qualified for the two regional libraries allowed by law. In addition, many thousands of federal government documents are never even included in the distribution to the depository system.

Francis Buckley, documents specialist at the Detroit Public Library, estimated a few years ago that the annual cost of maintaining that library's extensive depository holdings is $136,000. This is exclusive of the cost of space consisting of some 2,820 shelves required to house the collection. Detroit's obligations as a regional depository, which includes reference and interlibrary loan requests from selective depository libraries, adds another $5,670 a year to their expenses, again exclusive of space.

But maintaining a depository collection is only the tip of the iceberg when it comes to providing the public with a comprehensive collection of information by and about the United States

Government. The Detroit Public Library also acquires, either free or through purchase, various federal documents that do not find their way into the depository network. These include, for example, documents from the National Aeronautics and Space Administration, the Atomic Energy Commission, and 95 per cent of the papers distributed by the Department of Commerce's National Technical Information Service (NTIS), which is the central source for the sale of government-sponsored research and development reports and other government analyses prepared by federal agencies, their contractors or grantees. (The NTIS information collection exceeds 680,000 titles.) Also beyond the depository network are the documents of the Educational Resources Information Center (ERIC), which gathers, abstracts, and announces government publications resulting from projects supported by the National Institute of Education, the U.S. Office of Education, and other government agencies with similar interests.

Because so many government agencies and committees are lax about sending along publications to the Government Printing Office for deposit (the Central Intelligence Agency, for instance, makes almost nothing available), the Detroit Public Library, along with more than 150 other depository libraries, pays membership fees to the "Documents Expediting Project" at the Library of Congress, whose task is to canvass the various agencies for documents that have not been sent to the Government Printing Office for deposit. Detroit spends an additional $73,000 a year in staff, maintenance, and acquisition of these additional government documents.

A collection of documents without indices to provide access to the information in them is virtually useless. Therefore, the Detroit Public Library also pays $7,000 a year for such tools as the Congressional Information Service Index, American Statistics Index, Congressional Quarterly Weekly Reports, Cumulative Subject Index to the Monthly Catalog, and so forth. Altogether, Mr. Buckley estimates that the Detroit Public Library's role in making "government publications available for the free use of the general public" costs more than $222,000 a year, a cost borne entirely by state and local funds with no federal help at all.

The great flaw in the depository library concept is that the publications which the federal government supplies are not "free." They impose a heavy financial drain on the libraries that receive them and are conscientious about making them available to the public, which must be met *not* out of federal operating funds, but out of increasingly scarce state and local funds. What the federal government is actually doing by this program is creating an additional burden of millions of dollars on already financially hard-pressed libraries. Instead of providing for the free use of this invaluable informational material, congressional policy of providing vast quantities of government publications without the means to process them properly is actually helping to shorten the hours of library operation and force layoffs because of the extra financial drain.

A 1976 federal inspection report on deposition libraries noted the impact of local budget cutbacks on user access to government publications.

> All this is bad enough for those libraries which did manage to upgrade service during the last decade. But for those which didn't—and the documents area was often the last to be considered for upgrading—the situation encountered by inspectors is bleak. The person charged with looking after the depository collection is frequently in a near state of despair at trying to manage so much material and also attempting to provide service for demanding patrons.

Clearly a major overhaul of the whole approach to distributing government publications is long overdue.

PUBLIC LIBRARIES AND
THE INFORMED CITIZEN

> "A popular Government without popular information, or the means of acquiring it, is but a Prologue to a Farce or a Tragedy; or perhaps both. Knowledge will forever govern ignorance: And a people who mean to be their own Governors, must arm themselves with the power which knowledge gives."
>
> James Madison, *August 4, 1822, letter to W. T. Barry*

From its founding, the basic principle of American democracy has been informed citizen participation in the running of popular government. Freedom of speech and freedom of the press are only parts of the larger concept—a free trade of ideas in the marketplace from which the nation derives its strength. The primary storehouse of these ideas is an institution we all take for granted—the free public library. The public library is the nation's memory. It collects and stores up the information on which future decisions must be made—information for individual citizens, for authors of books and articles on current issues, for government researchers, social scientists, and journalists.

Increasingly, public libraries have taken on the responsibility of serving as depositories for state and local government documents as the importance of these governmental entities have gained increased recognition. No level of government today is exempt from pressure for information. People want and need to receive information on local and state government decisions which will influence the conduct and quality of their lives. Citizens, singly and in well-organized groups (many of whom learned advocacy skills in library-sponsored workshops), concern themselves with water quality, land use, consumer fraud, the provision of social services. The rapid proliferation of "sunshine" laws, which have opened up the conduct of official business to public scrutiny, is just one manifestation of the public demand to know what the government is doing.

Some local governments have learned that they can save time, space, and printing costs by using the local public library as the place where citizens and pressure groups can consult council minutes, local ordinances, zoning maps, and budget documents. Often the library is open longer hours or more convenient hours than government offices. And by nature it is equipped to give suitable storage space to older minutes, reports, maps, and other items that should be preserved for historical reasons. In most instances there are no ordinances providing for the deposit of local documents in the library, similar to state and federal depository laws. Conscientious librarians therefore must often be physically present in City Hall in order to obtain documents as they are released. The Madison (Wisconsin) Public Library solves the problem by placing its Municipal Reference Service right next to the elevator in the building where most of the city of Madison and Dane County offices are located. The service, which is operated as a branch of the Madison Public Library, responds to reference and information needs of both city and county employees and also helps the general public obtain information about Madison and Dane County governments. The branch maintains an extensive file of local documents, but, in addition, Ann Waidelich, Madison's municipal reference librarian, finds that by establishing a cooperative working relationship with city officials, she is better able to help the public. "We try to point people in the right direction, introduce them to the right people, and make the initial inquiries for them."

Energetic and imaginative librarians are finding many ways to get information on state and local government activities to the public. In Iowa, librarians obtain quick answers for patrons with legislative questions via a toll free line to the Iowa House of Representatives. A St. Louis Public Library "legislative hot line" was established in 1972 in response to citizen requests to give information beyond what television, radio, and newspapers provide—answering questions on the status of Missouri House and Senate bills, the time and place of hearings, and so on. When the Missouri legislature is not in session, the hot line provides information on bill signing, effective dates of legislation, the work of interim committees. Since the library is also a depository for state publications, state budgets, annual reports, appropriations data, statutes, manuals, and statistics of various state agencies, commissions, and departments, community information is always at hand for public use.

Public libraries often take affirmative steps to help the electorate get to know the political candidates, learn about the issues, and even register voters. The Hennepin County Library of Edina, Minnesota, taped the 1976 television debates of the presidential and vice-presidential candidates and made them available to the public for checkout. The Pickens County Library of Easley, South Carolina, held a three-hour "meeting the candidates rap-session" with the aim of giving the voters and candidates for County Council an opportunity to discuss campaign issues on an informed basis. Prior to the meeting, the library had the candidates answer a questionnaire which formed the basis for a one-page summary it prepared on each candidate's qualifications and views on issues. Using its branch and bookmobile staff, the St. Louis Public Library handled 37 per cent of the city's voter registration in 1976.

Libraries frequently serve as catalysts for community interaction. Several years ago the Martin Luther King Library in Washington, D.C., held a "Town Meeting" on pending school decentralization, which brought together concerned citizens, community leaders, and students to discuss the controversial issue. In a cooperative community effort to increase environmental awareness, the Dallas Public Library conducted a workshop for environmentalists and librarians to explore ways in which the library could work with community organizations to make environmental information more available to everyone. The library also published a community resource guide to inform the public of the range of environmental problems and of the resources and projects directed toward solutions. The guide was distributed through major city newspapers.

Libraries in nine counties in California and Nevada's ecologically sensitive Lake Tahoe region have formed a Sierra Libraries Information Consortium with the primary purpose of making accessible to anyone involved in the process of determining land-use policy—the electorate, land developers, environmental researchers, and resource managers—the great mass of environmentally related technical material that has been collected by a multitude of federal, state, local, and bistate agencies, academic researchers, and private collectors. Particularly helpful are the workshops in the use of the technical materials conducted by librarians at the Consortium's resource center in Lake Tahoe.

In the fall of 1976, the Junior League of Tulsa (Oklahoma) joined forces with the Tulsa City-County Library to develop a Citizen Information Service. Located within the library and easily available to the public, the service provides information on issues of importance to the community. Its purpose: to improve the opportunities for individuals to make quality decisions concerning issues affecting their lives and their community. Flooding, capital improvements, energy, and balanced growth are a few of the subjects included in the service. In preparation for the program the library interviewed various leaders in the community—the mayor, commissioners, newspaper editors, citizens' groups—and asked them what were the decisions that Tulsa would have to make within the next two years. Out of a list of about ten issues, the library selected, as a beginning, the three key questions that were most always mentioned—flooding, capital improvements, and water quality standards.

The Tulsa library is now the official depository for all floodplain information and is also a depository for local government documents. ("The city never remembers to give the library a copy of every document printed," says Suzanne Boles, who is in charge of the Citizen Information Center. "What we have to do is be aware of what is happening and go over there and get it.")

The library can provide information and referral on such subjects as topology, zoning, engineering, urban development, hearings, insurance, proposed channel improvements, open space programs, and so forth. The service has been particularly helpful to potential homeowners who can check the library's maps to determine whether or not a particular house or a particular area had been flooded in earlier years.

Materials have been gathered from the U.S. Corps of Engineers, the Tulsa City Engineering Department, homeowners associations, and several individuals. It has been indexed according to subject matter by Junior League volunteers for quick and easy reference. Also indexed are all the clippings from the local paper that had to do with flooding since 1952. On file are video tapes of those segments of the weekly city commission meetings that deal with flooding. Symposia on the subject are also video-taped and filed by the library. The tapes are available for use either there in the library or in churches, schools, and other locations.

The Tulsa experience is a good example of the way public libraries can serve their constituents in supplying information on all aspects of critical current issues. The principle is an obvious one—better access to information means better informed citizens, and better informed citizens means better government. It is just as true today as it was in Madison's time.

CHAPTER 7 ✳✳✳✳✳✳✳✳✳✳✳✳✳✳✳✳✳✳✳✳✳✳✳✳✳✳✳✳✳✳✳✳✳✳✳

The Pursuit
of Happiness

Romano Mazzoli grew up in the little mountain village of Maniago in northern Italy. When he was a small child, the family home caught fire and he suffered extensive burns which left his face badly scarred. In 1914, shortly after he turned eleven, Romano's father moved his wife and children to the United States, so he could join a family-owned tile, terrazzo, and marble business in Louisville, Kentucky. Three months after they arrived in Louisville, the boy's father died. Romano was sent to live with relatives.

He went to the local public school where, because he could speak no English, he was placed in the first grade. His embarrassment at being a large boy among small children was compounded by his disfiguring facial scar. He felt himself a misfit, and even though he began to advance rapidly in school as he learned to read and speak English, his relatives took him out of school when he reached seventh grade and apprenticed him in the family business.

Romano Mazzoli had a strong native intelligence. He was dextrous, imaginative, ingenious, intuitive, and a tremendously hard worker. He soon mastered the difficult craft of laying tile, setting terrazzo and mosaics, erecting marble, and doing decorative plasterwork. Before long he was a master mechanic, and soon a job foreman. As the business expanded, Romano was sent out of town to run jobs in distant cities, where he stayed at the branch YMCA or a local rooming house. The time after work hours was spent reading whatever he could lay his hands on. He haunted the public library every place he went. He developed an interest in music. Simultaneously he began to develop self-confidence and a love for his adopted country.

Eventually Romano Mazzoli went into business for himself. By hard work and the support of a devoted wife, the business flourished. He earned enough to send his three children to school for the education he never had. He personally taught them to respect and love books and music.

Today one of those children is a member of the United States Congress, who proudly carries on his father's name—Representative Romano L. Mazzoli of the Third District of Kentucky. Congressman Mazzoli speaks feelingly of the impact of the public library on three generations of his family:

> Many times over the years, Dad told me that, in his judgment, he was "Americanized" by the free public library system in the city of Louisville. What Dad meant by this, of course, was that the libraries enabled him to gain the knowledge and the understanding and the appreciation of things around him which he did not acquire in the formal setting of a classroom. The acquisition of this body of knowledge—in the countless hours he spent in libraries around the country—gave Dad the confidence to open up to the world around him and to open up to himself. The free public library system enabled him—a man of few means—to grow socially and intellectually.
>
> I am sure that because of my dad's great love of books and of the printed word, I acquired a love of books: a love affair which continues to the present day.
>
> And, as I look around my son's room, I see that this respect for and love of the written word has been transferred from my father through me to my son. He is only a junior in high school, yet he subscribes to four classical book clubs and is acquiring valuable book sets which he will have and use all the days of his life.

When Thomas Jefferson wrote his poetic introduction to the Declaration of Independence, he singled out three "unalienable" rights with which we have been endowed: "Life, Liberty, and the Pursuit of Happiness." As the experience of the Mazzoli family so graphically shows, probably no institution contributes more to the citizen's Pursuit of Happiness than the nation's public libraries.

TIME ON OUR HANDS

In June 1975, Lou Harris and Associates conducted a public-opinion survey of a scientifically drawn sample designed to be representative of the population of the United States. The survey was conducted for the National Committee for Cultural Resources, and its purpose was to determine the American public's attitude toward the arts.

When asked how important they felt it was to have various cultural facilities easily accessible to their homes, the overwhelming majority of those who were interviewed placed the public library at the *top* of their list. These were the survey results:

——Eighty-eight per cent thought that it is important to have a public library easily accessible.

——Seventy-six per cent, a park or botanical garden.

——Seventy-five per cent, a community, neighborhood, or recreation center where people learn various arts or crafts.

——Seventy per cent, a movie theatre.

——Sixty-nine per cent, a museum with paintings and sculpture, or with scientific and historical exhibits.

——Sixty-five per cent, a theatre where plays or musicals are performed.

——Sixty-three per cent, a concert hall where music or opera is performed.

What is so startling about these figures is that while there has been a flurry of public drumbeating in recent years to provide more tax dollars for the support of museums, theatres, concert halls, and other facilities, it turns out that it is the old-shoe public library which the man on the street wants most to have nearby.

Smart business entrepreneurs have not missed out on the significance of this public desire for easily accessible library facilities. When the new town of Columbia, Maryland, was under construction in 1959, its developers ran full-page real estate ads in the *Washington Post* and *Baltimore Sun* stressing the availability of a free public library. The advertisements showed a photograph of a librarian reading a book to a group of small children, under a banner headline: "COLUMBIA HAS THREE-YEAR-OLD BOOKWORMS." The copy went on to assure prospective home buyers that "the library is located in the village center, along with the village's shops and other services. It is a part of the daily life of the community it serves."

Actually, the Lou Harris survey result should not be at all surprising, considering the revolutionary growth in free time people now have at their disposal. Tremendous shifts in the work life of the average man and woman have occurred during the past century, and leisure time has increased spectacularly. In the 1870s, the average work week was fifty-three hours. Today the average is close to forty hours—about thirteen hours less than a century ago and a gain for each individual worker of about 675 hours of free time a year.

Paid vacations and holidays, first extended to managers, officials, and professional workers, have spread throughout the work force. By 1968, office workers received an average of eight paid holidays a year, plant workers about 7.5. All workers, according to the Bureau of Labor Statistics, have averaged a total gain in leisure time over a century ago of roughly one month out of twelve.

Much of the gain in reduced working hours since 1960 is due to the increasing number of part-time employees, the growth of employment in trade and services, and the reduction in farm employment (where long working hours are inherent). A widening gap between years in the work force and total life expectancy also accounts for a significant portion of the growth in free time. These trends are expected to continue.

The pattern of leisure time is also changing. Rather than small bits of leisure added to each day, "lumps of leisure" are gaining favor. Retirement years represent one such lump. By 1980, only 22 per cent of men sixty-five and over are expected to be in the labor force, down 4 percentage points from 1968. Improvement in Social Security benefits and private pension plans enable increasing numbers of older workers to take retirement. The rearrangement of national holidays in order to increase the number of three-day weekends, plus longer vacations, also represent increasing lumps of leisure time. Advances are also being made toward the four-day week. In mid-1971, some seventy-five thousand workers in about six hundred firms throughout the United States were on a four-day week. The sabbatical—first established for college teachers in the 1880s and by 1963, adopted in the steel industry—is another form of leisure that is likely to become more extensive in the future, according to the U.S. Department of Labor.

Of course, not all time free of work is translated into leisure. An analysis of how people spend their time (published in 1973 by the U.S. Office of Management and Budget) shows that Americans average 5.1 hours of leisure a day. This compares with 4.7 hours a day of work for pay; 6.4 hours for personal and family care; and 7.6 hours for sleep. Housewives have the most leisure hours a day—5.9. The male professional and executive averages 4.7 hours of leisure a day, while the working white-collar woman has the least leisure time of all, 4.2 hours. How are people spending their new-found free time and how do libraries help?

THE HOME HANDYMAN, HOBBYIST, AND GARDENER

Increased leisure and the high cost of services has transformed Americans into a nation of handymen and practical hobbyists—we repair our own cars; make simple carpentry, plumbing, and electrical repairs in our homes; build patios and walkways; sew our own clothes; refinish furniture; grow our own vegetables. Thousands turn their hands to useful and aesthetically pleasing hobbies

—we make pottery and jewelry, weave and spin and carve and paint, and tend our own flower gardens. All these tasks take skill and know-how.

A recent *New York Times* spot check of public libraries across the country reported a steady, heavy demand for how-to-do-it books, with particular emphasis on home appliance repairs, automobile repairs, and craft skills. A Seattle librarian explained, "People can't afford repairmen, so they are taking out books on do-it-yourself plumbing, car repair, home improvements."

Requests for books on how-to-do *practically anything* have skyrocketed in recent years. "We've had a tremendous number of requests for books on how to keep milk goats," Althea McAleer, director of the Fairfax County (Virginia) main branch library, told a *Washington Star* reporter. "We have six copies of *Starting Right with Milk Goats* and we can't keep them on the shelf."

Books in Print lists some twenty pages of currently available books whose titles begin with the words *How To,* presumably only a portion of the total current crop of instructional books available on library shelves to fill hobbyists' needs.

Public libraries also maintain collections of repair manuals for specific models of cars, washing machines, and other major home appliances. Some libraries serve community needs by loaning an assortment of equipment and hand tools, small engine repair kits, sewing machines and dress patterns, appliance trucks, auto creepers, sanders, and routers. The Grosse Pointe (Michigan) library has a collection of all types of wrenches, metal shears, sanders, upholstery gadgets, sledgehammers, ceramic snippers, and even large power tools that are lent out on a library card. The tools and their maintenance are provided by the Rotary Club. Many libraries offer courses in such fields as auto repair, clock repair, TV repair, upholstering, and building solar-heating equipment.

Some libraries maintain a skills bank file—a list of people in the community who are knowledgeable in certain areas and are willing to share that expertise.

A librarian in Portland, Maine, was able to put a retiree in touch with a professional silversmith to help him master advanced jewelry-making techniques. The man had become interested in jewelry making through his interest in rock hounding, but the only formal instruction course available to him—metalwork at the Portland High School—did not teach casting. Studying the library's collection of books on stone setting and silver casting could only take him so far. The *Portland Evening Express* in reporting the incident observed, "There may be only one person in Portland who knows about the 'lost wax' process—but the library found him."

Gardening is another favorite free-time activity. Each year Americans spend more than three billion dollars on flowers, seeds, and potted plants. Books on gardening account for some of the publishing industry's biggest sellers in the how-to category. In 1975, Macmillan printed 150,000 copies of *128 Bulbs You Can Grow*. Even a small publisher, the Philadelphia-based Running Press, in that same year printed 30,000 copies of *Indoor Plants* and 24,000 of *Greenhouses*.

Public libraries respond to this interest not only by keeping shelves bulging with a wide assortment of books on gardening and related subjects, but in other ways as well: The Hennepin County (Minnesota) library lends soil sample packets; the Eisenhower Public Library, part of the Illinois Suburban Library System, has turned a next-door vacant lot into a community gardening project; and the Buffalo-Erie County (New York) Public Library recently held a one-day "plant exchange," at which several hundred rooted plants were traded.

TRAVEL

In terms of dollars spent, the single most important American recreation is travel, for which Americans spent four billion dollars in the United States in 1970, with another five billion for travel abroad. Over a million passports are issued each year for pleasure travel. Public libraries assist prospective travelers in all kinds of ways. Collections of guidebooks; books about history, people, art, and architecture; tapes and records that will supply at least a basic facility in the languages of foreign countries being visited are all waiting to be borrowed.

Not long ago in Maine, a retired couple in their sixties drove to the library in Portland from their home fifty miles away to seek materials on Spain, which they were planning to visit. There they found a librarian who had lived in Spain and who spoke fluent Spanish. Over a two-month period the couple came to Portland for regular sessions with the librarian. They were provided with beginning Spanish-language records and phrase and grammar books, as well as information on food, currency, car rentals, train travel, and how to obtain an international driver's license.

For those who are traveling closer to home, a number of libraries offer special services. The St. Louis Public Library maintains a travel hot line where callers can get the latest information about road conditions, statewide fishing conditions, special events. The Vigo County (Indiana) library gives out-of-town visitors information about Terre Haute museums, art galleries, parks, and historical homes. The Chester County (Pennsylvania) library has put together, with the help of two community groups, "A Driving Tour of the Brandywine Valley," an attractive brochure, and a cassette tape (both can be borrowed from the county's libraries). The sixty-mile tour includes commentary on architecture, conservation efforts, geography, and local and natural history, along with detailed driving instructions, plus the operating hours for museums and parks.

THE ARTS

Throughout the centuries, increased leisure and the development of the arts have gone hand in hand. Today in America people from all walks of life are visiting museums, going to the theatre, to concerts, to opera, and to dance performances in unprecedented numbers. A 1975 Harris poll disclosed that 78 million people visited museums of all kinds that year for an average of 7.1 times, of which 65 million visited art museums (4.0 times). In the field of the performing arts, 62 million Americans went to the theatre (for an average of 4.6 times); 27 million went to the opera or a concert (4.1 times); 24 million attended a dance performance (3.0 times).

Although the United States supports some 800 opera companies (amateur, college, and professional), 1,465 symphony orchestras (amateur, college, and professional), and 1,821 museums, in most communities the public library is the principal cultural resource, serving as art and music center, as well as the repository for books and periodicals.

Public libraries offer an amazing range of cultural services. Music collections in thousands of libraries include not only books —the heart of any collection—but scores, part books, and libretti. Many public libraries provide performance materials for soloists and small ensembles, advanced students, and accomplished laymen-hobbyists. Phonograph records are a routine item in public libraries, even in the smallest communities.

In 1973, two thirds of the Illinois library districts, most of which have populations under ten thousand, reported record collections ranging from one to over twelve thousand.

Professor Walter C. Allen, of the Graduate School of Library Science at the University of Illinois, recently examined the music and art services offered by a group of larger public libraries in the continental United States serving populations ranging from thirty-three thousand to almost three million. Most of them, he found, maintain collections of classical recordings in some form (discs, tapes, cassettes), but many also have recordings of current popular music (81 per cent), current jazz (75 per cent), rock and country-western (72.5 per cent). Playing equipment is also circulated by 14 per cent. Collections scanning the breadth of musical offerings were found throughout the libraries queried, regardless of the size of the communities they served—most had books on musical theory, harmony, and composition, as well as musical biographies and other reference books.

In addition to enormous collections of records and tapes which people may borrow to take out, many large public libraries also have built up archives of recorded performances by musicians of all periods, which are designated as reference copies not for circulation. Newark (New Jersey) Public Library's archives, for example, hold both traditional and classic as well as jazz, blues, pop and rock—altogether more than one thousand albums. The pop category begins with W. C. Handy and early jazz, and continues down to major postwar figures such as Elvis Presley, the Beatles, Bob Dylan, the Jackson Five, the Supremes, and many others. According to William J. Dane, supervising librarian of Newark's Art and Music Department, these albums are in such great demand that "visitors sometimes wait in line to use the ten listening machines."

To help small and medium-sized libraries establish good music collections, the Music Library Association's Continuing Education Committee publishes basic lists of reference books, scores, and recordings, and has a traveling sound-slide show which explains to librarians many of the basics of acquiring, processing, and circulating music materials.

In addition to offering collections of and about music, public libraries frequently provide actual concerts, usually recorded performances played in the library. A few libraries hold concerts outside the library, often in their own gardens. About a third of the larger public libraries surveyed by Professor Allen have listening rooms; most others have some sort of listening stations. Ten libraries have practice rooms, generally equipped with pianos.

Recent examples of live concerts held in libraries include:

Sunday-afternoon concerts performed by the Chicago Symphony Orchestra String Quartet.

A "Premiere Series" at the Hartford (Connecticut) Public Library featuring professional musicians in recitals which "premiere a new, unpublished piece of music." Artists have included soprano Josephine Graziano and pianist Richard Kessler.

Hartford also invites inner-city workers to bring their lunches to the library for "coffee concerts" featuring local performing artists who welcome the opportunity to perform before a live audience.

The Nashua (New Hampshire) Public Library holds country music concerts and Lake County (Indiana) Public Library has sponsored rock concerts.

Public library visual-art collections often contain art books, exhibition catalogues, catalogues of museum collections, and photographs—both as reproductions and as works of art. Some libraries offer videotapes, which can be viewed privately on a television monitor, such as Roy Lichtenstein discussing his painting technique; George Segal, sculpting; perhaps a series offering instruction in the playing of simple musical instruments; or slide collections (sometimes in sets accompanied by a script or tape such as Louise Nevelson describing her career and sculpture). Slides are available for people interested in art history, also for handicraft instruction, and to provide documentation of local artists' work and collectibles. There are also scores of films on such subjects as the paintings of Andrew Wyeth, the history of architecture, the art of glassmaking, pottery techniques, Rodin's sculpture, the Dance Theatre of Harlem, the career of actress Helen Hayes.

Circulating collections of framed art prints are also offered by many public libraries. Such lending services are generally offered by libraries serving populations from one hundred thousand to a million. Presumably the smaller libraries cannot afford the service, and larger cities often have museums which offer these services.

"The highly simplified life-styles of many young people seem to make a framed picture at 'home' an important supplement," says Hester Miller, head of Albuquerque Public Library's Fine and Performing Arts Department. Albuquerque has established a lending collection of framed pictures, both reproductions and originals (lithographs, etchings, engravings) as a memorial to its former chief librarian, Donald Riechmann, who had a personal interest in making such resources available. Cooperating with the library in this project has been the Tamarind Institute of Lithography at the University of New Mexico, as well as local galleries.

Many libraries mount exhibits relating to the arts, and some sponsor traveling shows.

Dance, too, is part of most library collections. Here can be found books ranging from Arthur Murray's *How to Become a Good Dancer,* to the Royal Academy of Dancing's *Beginning Ballet,* as well as instructional recordings for square and folk dances, ballet, modern, and other forms. The Chicago Public Library has a file of instructions for over one thousand different folk dances indexed by name, alternate name, and country or region of origin. Among the more unusual library activities is a professionally trained resident Afro-American Dance Company at the Montclair (New Jersey) Public Library, which tours the state in a van and station wagon performing at libraries and cultural institutions. The

Bridgeport (Connecticut) bookmobiles take the city's resident dance company around town for "street dancing" performances.

Public libraries in some areas provide portable videotaping equipment for library patrons, who, after learning how to use the equipment, can go out into the community and produce their own television shows. Brooklyn Public Library utilizes this equipment in its work with ghetto teen-agers. The Port Washington (New York) library loans portable video and film equipment and offers training sessions with professionals. The films that are made from the project become part of the library's collection. The Grand Rapids (Michigan) Public Library's young adult department holds an annual Amateur Filmmakers' Festival which showcases locally produced amateur films, and has sponsored a statewide competition open to any amateur filmmaker or filmmaking group.

The Toledo-Lucas County (Ohio) Public Library has a darkroom for the processing of black-and-white photographic film and prints. The Southdale-Hennepin Area (Minnesota) library gives photography buffs free access to the library's own darkroom facilities. Users armed with a library card, plus their own film, chemicals, photographic paper, and mounting board, can use all of the basic equipment needed to develop and print photos—trays, dryers, enlargers, thermometer, and so on.

Libraries are frequent sponsors of talks by well-known writers. The New Rochelle (New York) Public Library and the New Rochelle Council on the Arts have held a writers' lecture series with such authors as E. L. Doctorow, Francine du Plessix Gray, and Judith Rossner among the participating authors. The "Conversations with Writers" are held not only at the library but also at local churches and synagogues, schools, and community centers. Through a program of lectures at thirty-six public libraries, Illinois launched a program in 1975 to give greater visibility to Illinois writers. The Great Neck (New York) library sponsored lectures and an exhibit on famous resident F. Scott Fitzgerald.

A new poetry magazine is being produced with the aid of the Groton (Connecticut) Public Library which provides duplicating equipment, including an electronic stencil cutter that will reproduce halftones; and an editorial working center that permits any editor to stop by, write his comments on poetry submissions, and leave them for the next editor's reactions. The Groton library also works very closely with Seabury Players, a local theatre group, and at the request of the town manager has been conducting a survey to help determine the shape and function of a proposed Fine Arts Council.

A vivid picture of the type of public-library demands made by the general public in the field of music and art is reflected in the following list published in the January 1975 issue of *Library Trends* magazine. These are the areas where most user requests fall:

Music

1. Song collections of all kinds—popular, folk, art songs, and nostalgic, community, sacred, and ribald songs.

2. Theatre music, especially piano-vocal scores of standard repertory operas, "workshop" operas, most modern musical shows, with the associated librettos and scripts if available.

3. Miniature scores, representing the standard repertoire but not overlooking the twentieth century and the avant-garde, always with a view to what is within the community's production capability, what may turn up on a broadcast, what composers (Joplin or Pachelbel or Mahler) are in vogue on recordings.

4. Instructional method books for the popular instruments—guitar, recorder (more recently, the flute), zither, autoharp, dulcimer, mbira, even the piano and organ.

5. Standard literature for solo instruments—keyboard, string, and wind instruments—requiring considerable proficiency, hopefully in the best modern editions.

6. Some chamber music, not necessarily for "standard" combinations.

Visual Arts

1. All kinds of identification manuals—for silver, porcelain, glass, furniture, artists.

2. All kinds of handicraft books—how-to-do-it, idea, and pattern books.

3. Art techniques—how to draw, how to paint in various media, how to sculpt, how to weave, knit, and knot.

4. Home plan books and blueprint catalogues.

5. Collecting manuals—price and auction information.

6. Interior decoration.

7. Information about museums and sources of art reproductions.

8. Information on local and ethnic art.

Performing Arts

1. All kinds of biographical material.

2. Address information—where to write to an old or new favorite performer, how to get in touch with personal and business agents.

3. All kinds of credit information—who played what part in which play; who wrote what and what it was based on and who made it popular, the revival or remake or musicalization or serialization as well as the original.

4. All kinds of genre information—pop music styles, dances of various periods, monster and Western movies.

5. Trade information—polls, grosses, charts, ratings.

6. Calendar information—what is going to be, what is going to happen where and when, sometimes in a historical perspective.

7. Nostalgia information—the typical performance matter and style of recent decades, the charms of which seem ever more compelling.

8. Publisher and publishing information—especially as it relates to sources for musical scores, less readily available recordings, and performance rights.

THE SEARCH FOR KNOWLEDGE

There probably is no trait more typically American than the desire for finding things out. People want to know what makes everything tick. People want to know how they can make themselves more interesting, more beautiful, more intelligent, more well-to-do. People want knowledge because of what it can do for them, and also for the sheer joy of the quest itself. Whatever the motivation, the public library is home to the intellectually curious.

Local History

There is hardly a public library anywhere in the country that does not have at least one shelf of materials on local history. Stimulated by the recent U.S. Bicentennial, business in the local-history departments has been booming. Likewise, the impact of the Alex Haley best-seller *Roots* has stimulated great interest in tracing family history. The St. Louis Public Library has put together a list of reference sources for the beginner in the field, plus a list of addresses for family records research, and a brief guide to use of the library's genealogy and local history collection. The Salem (Massachusetts) Public Library now offers an eight-week course in genealogy.

Some library local-history programs are quite ambitious. For the past several years Boston library users have had the opportunity to learn about their city through an instruction program entitled "Boston and the Urban Environment," funded by a National Endowment for the Humanities' (NEH) Learning Library grant. The eight-to-ten-week course includes lectures, field trips, and individual study guidance. Topics have included "The Way We Really Live: Social Changes in Metropolitan Boston since 1920," conducted by Sam Bass Warner, Jr., a Boston University professor known for his studies of social change in the inner city; "Bibles,

Brahmins and Bosses: Leadership in the Boston Community," conducted by Thomas O'Connor of Boston College; "Boston Architecture: from First Town House to New City Hall," by Professor Gerald Bernstein of Brandeis University. Professor Bernstein's lectures, limited to fifty persons, have been so popular that people regularly stood in line hoping to obtain last-minute seats. When the architect of Boston's new City Hall came as a guest lecturer, the library's four-hundred-seat lecture hall was not large enough to hold all who wanted to attend. "We have had standing room only for all of the programs," reports Boston's assistant library director, Y. T. Feng.

Library lecturers are drawn from the Boston area and beyond— from Tufts, Brandeis, and Boston universities, MIT, the Boston Museum of Fine Arts, Worchester Polytechnic, and Rhode Island College. The latter college's chairman of black studies conducted a series of lectures—to be published as a book by the library—entitled "Boston's Black Letters: from Phillis Wheatley to W. E. B. du Bois."

An actress who attended the series on "Bibles, Brahmins and Bosses" became so intrigued with the story of Angelina Grimké Weld, wife of the abolitionist Theodore Dwight Weld, that she launched into further research at the library and then wrote an educational play, *Freedom and Angelina,* which has already been performed in twenty-five libraries in eastern Massachusetts.

THE ODDBALLS

People who utilize public-library collections for their personal pursuit of happiness number in the millions. Their search is for pleasure and enjoyment, and they find it in full measure. But here and there among the millions of users of these resources is the occasional oddball who is using the library for a serious special purpose of his own.

Perhaps that purpose may be the creation of new art forms for future enjoyment.

ITEM: Agnes de Mille, the choreographer and dancer who brought the ballet form to musical comedy in *Oklahoma!* and thereafter in such musicals as *Bloomer Girl, Carousel, Brigadoon,* has said that "The Dance Collection of The New York Public Library is known throughout the world as the best and most serviceable archive of its kind. . . . Chances are that the revival of any work is dependent on access to the Dance Collection." When Soviet ballerina Natalia Makarova came to the United States in 1970, she prepared herself for performances with the American Ballet Theatre by studying at length the films in the NYPL Dance Collection.

ITEM: Louis Sheaffer, author of the Pulitzer prize-winning biography *O'Neill, Son and Playwright,* wrote in the book's acknowledgment, "The matter for this book was amassed with the generous help of many persons, libraries, official agencies, and institutions. . . . In listing libraries first among the groups, I pay tribute to their being a writer-researcher's indispensable ally and support . . . the people who work for libraries are among the worthiest members of our society."

ITEM: Writer David McCullough, who recently completed five years of research for his Pulitzer prize-winning *The Path Between the Seas: The Creation of the Panama Canal,* wrote that "My own work would be quite impossible without [public libraries] and the regard I have for the librarians could not be higher. They are *the* great public servants. The crying shame is that the public, including the so-called educated public, seems to have little or no conception of how much the library system can make available."

ITEM: *The New Yorker* cartoonist Charles Addams; theatre caricaturist Al Hirschfeld; fashion designers Vera, Donald Brooks, and the late Norman Norell; and scores of men and women who design scenery, costumes, and lighting effects for the theatre, opera, and ballet regularly consult the two million clippings from books and magazines in the NYPL's Picture Collection.

ITEM: John Jakes, whose series of richly detailed historical novels have sold over sixteen million copies, recently told a *Wall Street Journal* reporter that he draws most of his research from the historical accounts, diaries, old newspapers, and other source materials "among the one million volumes at the Dayton and Montgomery County [Ohio] Public Library."

The value of the special collections of the nation's public libraries lies not simply in the direct pleasure they give to countless users, but also in the indirect impact they have on the creations of particular library users of exceptional capacity. No one can really tell who these intent library users are, or where they are going. President Harry S. Truman once told the president of the American Library Association, "Everything I know—except my law—I learned through the public library." Truman is the only President in this century who never attended college. By the time he was fourteen, he had read every single book in the Independence Public Library. Many librarians take due note of the fact that in any group of library users there may well be a future President of the United States.

CHAPTER 8 ✶✶✶✶✶✶✶✶✶✶✶✶✶✶✶✶✶✶✶✶✶✶✶✶✶✶✶✶✶✶✶✶✶✶✶

New Horizons for Older Americans

Leroy R. Paige made sports history in 1948 when he became the first black pitcher in major league baseball. In 1965, he made history again by becoming the oldest player in the major leagues, pitching for Kansas City when he was almost sixty.

"Satchel" Paige had a colorful personality which was reflected in his formula for staying young:

1. Avoid fried meats which angry up the blood.

2. If your stomach disputes you, lie down and pacify it with cool thoughts.

3. Keep the juices flowing by jangling around gently as you move.

4. Go very lightly on the vices, such as carrying on in society. The social ramble ain't restful.

5. Avoid running at all times.

6. Don't look back. Something might be gaining on you.

Mr. Paige might have added:

7. Keep your mind alert and alive by visiting your public library regularly.

That is exactly what countless other senior citizens do to fill up their weeks and months. And they love it, because it, too, helps keep them young.

Take Elsie Levy. At seventy-one, she lives alone in a small apartment in the center of Manhattan. Her eyesight and hearing are sound, and, although somewhat frail, she gets around the city quite well. Her problem is money. Like the majority of older women, she is poor. The Social Security checks and small pension she has received since her retirement from a merchandising firm in 1969 hardly cover the barest necessities. "I thought I would be able to manage," she says. "My wants are very simple. Gradually, you just run out of money." Once favorite activities—tickets to the opera, to concerts, to the theatre, classes at a nearby university— must now remain joys of the past.

Instead, Elsie Levy spends a lot of her time at the Muhlenberg Branch of the New York Public Library, a block from her apartment. She can go to the library as frequently as she likes and can borrow as many books as she can carry home. "I find the library essential to my well-being. I really don't know what I would do without it," she says. She loads up with biographies, novels, mysteries, and suspense stories. She lingers to read *The New Yorker* magazine and other magazines she can no longer afford to buy. When a playwright who lives in her neighborhood held a play-reading course at the library, she joined in. She had been an actress in her youth and "loved reading the plays out loud and enjoyed the feeling of acting again."

There are millions of Elsie Levys in America today. They are the "new poor," men and women living in retirement on severely reduced incomes. In 1900, the man or woman who lived beyond the age of fifty was the exception. At that time, only 3 per cent of the population lived to be over sixty-five; now 10 per cent have already marked their sixty-fifth birthday, more than twenty-two million persons. By the end of this century, the U.S. Census Bureau expects that number to have swelled to more than thirty million. Although the elderly now account for 10 per cent of the population, they account for 25 per cent of the poor. Clearly, free library service in their communities is vital to the growing numbers of older Americans.

Of paramount significance in gauging public-library use by this growing segment of the population is the rising level of educational attainment of the aging. In study after study, educational level emerges as the most important single factor affecting increased adult use of the American public library.

As persons with more education move into older age groups, the level of educational attainment increases for the entire adult population. The proportion of high school graduates among those sixty-five and older was only 18 per cent as recently as 1959. By 1975, half of those sixty-five and over had completed more than nine years of school (while over half of all adults twenty-five and over had completed twelve years of school or more). Within fifteen years (1990), nearly half will be high school graduates.

Many older adults who regularly use libraries are "invisible" patrons who hold no library cards and never charge out books. Their use of the library is usually unrecorded. But for them, the library may be their most important resource, providing an opportunity to escape the confinement of their rooms, to sit and read comfortably among other people in a pleasant atmosphere. One woman in an eastern city recently wrote:

> Since retirement I have become dependent on the public library for mental stimulation. I am alone, a senior citizen, so I tell you this as typical of the plight of many a senior citizen. In the short span of six months, a close friend moved to Florida, another friend passed away, a close relative moved out of the state, a close relative passed away. Do you know what a library does for such as I? I can't do without the book discussions. They are stimulating, exciting, challenging, listening and learning and exchanging thoughts, being with people who are alive and alert. To me, it is like getting out in the fresh air, like a tonic, like a medicine, giving me the strength to go on.

Neighborhood influences often play an important role in the special meaning of particular libraries to particular older citizens.

Every day a number of elderly gentlemen come to the Seward Park Branch Library in Manhattan to spend a few hours reading the Yiddish-language *Jewish Daily Forward*. Some of the men travel long distances by subway from Brooklyn or the Bronx to return to the library of their childhood and to be with their old friends. The Seward Park Branch has a good collection of Yiddish and Hebrew books—de Maupassant in Yiddish moves well—and the librarian is likely to find herself ordering Russian-language editions of Pushkin and other classics for her elderly patrons. Rarely do these users take books out of the library. "They worry about being responsible for books that might be lost or stolen," says the librarian. "They can't pay for a book if it disappears."

Not many blocks west of the Seward Park Branch sits the pillared facade of the Chatham Square Library in the heart of Chinatown. Here the favorite newspaper is the *Sing Tao Jih Pao,* but the patterns of library use by the elderly are similar to those at Seward Park. Farther north in Greenwich Village elderly residents seek out the Jefferson Market Branch—the building is air conditioned in summer, heated in winter, and is a safe place to be. In other neighborhoods, such as the one served by the Webster Branch on the Upper East Side, the elderly come by for half an hour, take out the large-print books, look over the new acquisitions, stay a bit longer on Thursdays when the new *Time* and *Newsweek* come in.

CONTINUING EDUCATION FOR THE ELDERLY

At the age of sixty-three, Paul Kinchen enrolled in Case Western Reserve University and began his master's degree program in education. He graduated in January 1975, and is now the coordinator of Senior Citizens Activities at Cuyahoga County Community College in Cleveland. Mr. Kinchen lectured not long ago before the Cleveland Public Library's Live Long and Like It Club on the subject "You're Never Too Old To Learn." He told the members about legislation that provided financial and educational assistance to persons sixty and over who wish to attend state universities and colleges. He talked about the misconceptions and myths concerning older senior citizens. He told them about his program at Cuyahoga Community College which enrolls persons sixty years and older into state colleges and universities.

Paul Kinchen personifies the change in thinking that has occurred in this country since the Live Long and Like It Club was established in 1946 under the leadership of Fern Long and Clara Lucioli. The club was dedicated to the then rather novel idea that attention should be paid to the educational needs of older people as well as to requirements of shelter and food. It also marked a milestone in the development of library services because it introduced the idea of service to the elderly, a segment of the population hitherto not considered a special group.

Now, three decades later, there is widespread recognition that older Americans require a broad range of educational services to assist them in life-change situations and to find new outlets for their skills and interests. The "twilight years" notion that older adults have no capacity for continued mental growth or social contribution has largely been dispelled. Psychosocial research has proved without a doubt that age has nothing to do with intellectual acuity. Older people may not think as quickly as they once did, but their conclusions are just as sound and their store of information and vocabularies can grow indefinitely.

Kathlyn Adams, outreach consultant at the Monroe County (New York) Public Library in Rochester, has helped senior citizens learn the techniques of advocacy on behalf of themselves. Their advocacy group, Citizen Leaders for Action in Rochester (CLAR), has tackled questions relating to Social Security legislation, nursing homes, and property tax exemptions, and presented their group's views to local, state, and federal officials. Through CLAR's effort, the New York State Office for the Aging is starting a program of volunteer ombudsmen familiar with arbitration procedures to work in nursing homes in Rochester to help patients and staff as well as their families.

Members of the local chapter of the American Association of Retired Persons conduct workshops at the library at Grand Prairie, Texas, dealing with defensive driving, health and safety, nutrition, budget guidance, income tax aid, and "over 55" art exhibits. At the Brighton Beach Branch of the Brooklyn Public Library, nurses from nearby Coney Island Hospital lecture on personal health—diabetes, hypertension, nutrition.

Librarians work with nearby community colleges to provide special courses for the elderly. In Manhattan and the Bronx in

New York City, older people in the neighborhood participate in selecting the subject matter of the courses to be held in their libraries. These have ranged from sex and the older adult to fine arts to discussion of broad social issues of the day.

No one knows exactly how many older adults are enrolled in courses sponsored by colleges and universities. It is likely, however, that there are thousands attending classes each year who—because of current data collection methods—never show up in the educational statistics. Based on the experience of some 212 institutions that keep data on their older student enrollment, the Academy for Educational Development estimates that enrollment increased by nearly 2,600 per cent during the five-year period from 1970 to 1975.

A Louis Harris survey in 1975 found that 400,000 older people were currently enrolled in an educational institution or taking courses. (This amounts to 2 per cent of those sixty-five and over; 5 per cent of the forty-to-sixty-four-age group are so enrolled.) Senior-citizen enrollment ranges from the college or university level (24 per cent), to adult educational schools, church schools, high schools, and correspondence schools. An overwhelming majority of senior-citizen students (76 per cent) say they are taking courses to expand general knowledge about some field or hobby.

Colleges are making it easier for older adults to take their courses. According to a telephone survey conducted by the staff of the Academy for Educational Development at the close of 1976, twenty-seven states had passed legislation or adopted educational policies enabling their older citizens to take courses at public colleges and universities, either without the payment of tuition or for payment of greatly reduced charges. The academy estimates that one out of four colleges and universities in the United States has reduced tuition charges for older Americans.

Contrary to popular opinion, courses in academic subjects are the most popular among older adults; courses having to do with hobbies and recreation run a close second; with public information and consumer education next in line. The nine most popular single subjects were in history (in all its myriad forms, from world to local), psychology, health, foreign languages (especially Spanish), literature, painting, creative writing, religion, needlework. But whatever the subjects taken, more older adults in the nation's colleges and schools means more older adults in the nation's public libraries. Adult students are known to be heavy and demanding public-library patrons.

INFORMATION AND REFERRAL SERVICES FOR OLDER CITIZENS

"I am a sixty-two-year-old widow living on Social Security benefits of $175 a month, am I entitled to get food stamps?"

"The power company is going to shut off my electricity because my bill is overdue, what can I do?"

Public-library information and referral services in many communities are answering these questions, and thousands more like them, for older Americans every day.

Poor eyesight, poor hearing, physical frailty, educational handicaps—all interfere with the older person's ability to obtain information to cope with the complexities of modern living. Half of all elderly Americans—rich and poor—have no more than a high school education. Reduced income plunges the older person into a snarl of social services—food stamps, rent supplements, supplemental security income, Medicaid, Meals on Wheels, nutrition centers, reduced bus fares. An Urban Institute study recently concluded that the great majority of the elderly poor have at most an eighth-grade reading level, while government-prescribed procedures for many social-welfare programs require substantially higher levels of reading skill and achievement. A sampling of eighty-one official documents found only 11 per cent judged comprehensible to those with eighth-grade skills. A great many of the forms required college-reading-level comprehension. Not surprisingly, the Urban Institute suggests that this mismatch between a client's ability to read and welfare agencies' demands for literacy of its clients discourages persons eligible for benefits from enrolling, causes inequity in the distribution of benefits among enrollees, and leads to high agency error rates. For people who had led self-sufficient, dignified lives, the psychological anguish of attempting to cope can be devastating. The opportunity to turn for needed information to a public library, therefore, can sometimes make an important difference.

The Plainedge (New York) Public Library serves a middle-class population of just under twenty-five thousand. Like many suburban communities, the proportion of elderly in the community is sizable—about 10 per cent—and growing rapidly. The Plainedge Public Library publishes a newsletter for the elderly called *Discovery,* which is mailed to the home of every over-sixty resident in the community. *Discovery* tells the recipient about TOTE, the new, free Red Cross-provided, door-to-door transportation for seniors who are physically or financially unable to use other means of transportation for medical services, visits to nutrition sites, and other priority services. (The library mans the telephone end of this service for the Red Cross.) It tells them about the volunteer-run FISH program that supplies emergency transportation, service for shut-ins, and emergency help in the home. (The library mans this phone also.) It tells them about the Nassau County Bar Association's Lawyer Referral Program set up to provide legal consultation for senior citizens at nominal fees; reprints useful tax information from a Citibank newsletter; carries a short article advising people what they should do before buying a hearing aid; and includes names, addresses, and phone numbers of clinics where hearing-aid professionals can be found. It explains in simple, clear detail how to determine whether or not you are eligible for food stamps. *Discovery,* however, is more than a useful fact sheet. By manning the phones for both the TOTE and FISH services, the library's information and referral staffs are often able to provide callers with links to additional needed services.

Starting in 1974, the Tulsa (Oklahoma) City-County Public Library initiated a major information and referral service exclusively for senior citizens in their central library and in the two adjoining rural counties of Creek and Osage. Tulsa's central library service was expanded to become a total community information and referral service in September 1977, but service in the two rural counties continued to be exclusively for older adults. The program receives funding under Title III of the Older Americans Act, part of the recent push at the federal and state levels to increase services for the elderly.

Tulsa's publicity for the program was designed especially to reach senior citizens—it was printed in large print; the coordinator of the program spent an enormous amount of time going to senior centers and to nutrition sites with a slide show to demonstrate the service. A seemingly small thing turned out to be an effective way of bringing older adults into the city's library for the first time— the library became issuing agent for the senior-discount bus pass in Tulsa. Since all the city buses stop at the library, this brought many new people into the building and introduced them to the resources of the library.

In the first full month of operation, the Tulsa service logged just over a hundred telephone and walk-in contacts. By the end of three years, the service was receiving six to seven hundred inquiries a month. "Requests for transportation are probably three-to-one the main inquiry we receive," explains Phyllis Jobe, who runs the Tulsa operation. "Recreation and involvement of some kind is probably the second largest request." The city has a good system of senior centers, a good recreation program in community schools, and the Park Department is increasingly engaged in senior programming. Other major subjects of inquiry by older citizens have been housing, nutrition, financial assistance, utility bill problems, and food stamps. The library staff has found a three-way phone particularly helpful in serving the elderly—the librarian can stay on the phone with the older person to make sure he or she gets the needed service from the referral agency.

The Tulsa librarians have found, as have librarians in other cities, that their information and referral services propel them into taking on affirmative programs to solve specific service needs. Opel Brewer, the Tulsa program's coordinator, has worked with the city's dentists to get a low-cost denture program underway. Ms. Brewer has also helped organize the Tulsa Coalition for Older People, an advocacy group for which the library provides a meeting room, a place to distribute literature, a bulletin board, and, of course, research materials such as names of legislators, status of bills, and so forth. The coalition is currently working to bring about newspaper advertising of eyeglasses so that prices can become more competitive.

Opel Brewer plays a large part in training the information and referral component in senior centers and nutrition sites all over the three counties her library serves. Outreach workers, center coordinators, nutrition site managers—the entire staff of senior centers and nutrition sites are all brought into the library for I&R training to make sure they understand the concept. As new centers get started, the Tulsa I&R team goes in and provides the technical assistance for setting up the resource file and plugs them into the main information centers in their county; all the centers are connected on a toll-free line.

The information and referral staffs in the highly rural Osage County and Creek County libraries had to get out and work door-to-door publicizing their service. Their goal has been to help older people live independently and safely in their own homes for as long as possible. Often they find that counseling, encouragement, and support are all a person needs to live a more abundant life. Some contacts have been a simple matter of information or referral; others have required a long-term commitment by the I&R staff.

Coordination with other agencies has proved to be an important function of I&R. The Creek County staff has worked closely with the Welfare Department's nontechnical medical-care program. A list of in-home providers is kept in the I&R office and elderly people needing home care are helped to apply for this assistance. With just a few hours of care each day, many older people have been able to stay securely in their own homes, the library discovered. "A great many older people reject anything to do with 'welfare,'" report the Creek County workers, "but personal attention from the staff of the rural I&R and trust in their activities often makes 'acceptable' services the elderly might not otherwise accept." The library staff also helps its senior clients cope with printed forms from social-service agencies. Many of these forms seem obscure to older people; they frequently think that a form means their assistance has ended. They do not always understand the terms used. Some, because of poor eyesight, actually cannot see the form.

Among the many other services provided to the elderly by library personnel in Creek County are:

Reading and writing letters for people who can do neither, typing copies of recipes for women who want to share, counseling a retarded woman, sacking and distributing seeds donated by the Community Action Program, making a meat loaf for a man who had just had all his teeth extracted, gearing up several agencies to provide help for burned-out families in the area.

Both Osage and Creek counties lack many of the social-service agencies that a larger county would have, and this has meant that the I&R staffs have worked with Key Club boys, women's groups, and other organizations to get many things done for senior citizens. Concludes Phyllis Jobe, "It should be apparent that the nature of I&R becomes, by necessity, different as the function moves from the metropolitan to the rural setting." Nevertheless, although the level of service may be much more personal, "the basic principles are the same: accurate information, trustworthiness, coordination and cooperation between agencies, accessibility."

SENIOR CITIZENS AS LIBRARY RESOURCES

At the age of fifty-seven, Mrs. Elsie Gillingham, widow of a police officer, went to work as a librarian clerk at the Sandusky, (Ohio) Public Library. It was her first paying job. She now works twenty hours a week at the minimum wage under the federally funded Senior Community Service Project, which provides employment in needed community services, like libraries, for people over fifty-five whose incomes place them below the poverty line. Mrs. Gillingham was ineligible to receive Social Security and her only source of income was a small pension from her husband's job. She started her work at the library thinking she was not qualified to do anything. The training she received, however, soon boosted her confidence and now, in addition to holding down the job, she is going to school to learn additional skills. Senior aides like Mrs. Gillingham are found in public libraries in a large percentage of the forty-eight communities where SCSEP projects are located, according to the National Council on the Aging, which administers the program.

The Cleveland Public Library has run workshops to train older volunteers—members of Foster Grandparents, for example—so that they can conduct children's story hours in libraries. In Newton, Kansas, the public library uses older adults as a resource for children's interest groups, mothers' discussion seminars, and adult literature groups, and finds that the interaction has been stimulating for all involved. Sometimes senior citizens are cultivated as research resources. One Milwaukee shut-in has compiled a list of titles about Ireland and is systematically making her way through them. "When she has completed reading the books on her list," a librarian explains, "we believe she will be an unusually expert source of information about Ireland's literature, people, and customs."

Literacy programs draw on older persons to serve as tutors. At the Brooklyn Public Library more than a third of the volunteer tutors are over sixty years of age.

As part of its recreational and educational program, the Monroe County (New York) Public Library provides live entertainers to senior centers—magicians, pianists, a woman who displays and talks about her extensive doll collection—all of them over sixty, all of them volunteers. Demand for these performers has been so great that the library maintains a "skills bank" file so that other agencies may draw on the performers' services.

For several weeks prior to April 15 each year, retired accountants, who are members of the American Association for Retired Persons and are specially trained by the Internal Revenue Service, serve as volunteers to help elderly citizens fill out their tax returns in thousands of public libraries across the country.

MEETING SPECIAL NEEDS

What are libraries doing to help meet the special needs of this growing sector of American society? Weakening eyesight, physical frailty, loss of hearing, the psychological problems of isolation from the mainstream of American life are inevitably part of the aging process. Various libraries supply a variety of special materials to help overcome these isolating barriers.

Large-print Books

Elderly people who have difficulty reading normal-size print can usually find on the shelves of their local public library a collection of attractively designed, easy-to-read large-print editions of best sellers, gothics, romances, Westerns, biographies, how-to books—just about every category of publication imaginable. Many libraries also carry the special large-print weekly edition of *The New York Times* and the large-print edition of *Reader's Digest*.

The availability of large-print materials is revolutionizing public-library service to the elderly, a revolution largely stimulated by librarians themselves. Most public libraries in this country had none of these materials as recently as ten years ago. Production of large-print books was started as a nonprofit operation in the 1950s in England by Sir Fred Thorpe of Ulverscroft Books. The early Ulverscroft and other large-print books ran to out-of-copyright titles like *Ivanhoe* and *Silas Marner* and showed remarkably little understanding of the potential market. A federally funded project at the Donnell Branch of the New York Public Library in the late 1960s demonstrated that readers most wanted current popular titles. "They wanted the same things that everyone else was reading, preferably at the same time," recalls Richard Tirotta, one of the librarians involved in the project. Today, G. K. Hall, the primary publisher of large-print books in America, has almost achieved that immediacy.

An elderly reader can find on library shelves, usually within six months of original publication, such titles as John Le Carré's *The Honourable Schoolboy* and Saul Bellow's *To Jerusalem and Back*. Because the books are completely reset in 18-point type, their size is the same as any standard trade book, which means that longer volumes—*The Honourable Schoolboy,* for example—must be printed in two volumes. These books are expensive to produce—the two volumes of the Le Carré best seller costs $18.95, and even paperback editions of large-print books typically run anywhere from $9 to $14. They are therefore beyond the personal means of the great majority of their elderly readers and simply would not be produced were it not for the market made possible by the public libraries.

The publishers of large-print books work very closely with librarians, and depend on them to let them know what readers ask for, and also whether the books are physically acceptable. Explains Edward F. McCartan of John Curley and Associates, "We just changed our cover material to a sturdier one and our paper also in direct response to the feedback we get from librarians. We use very lightweight paper—to keep the bulk of the books down—and of course when you get into lightweight paper you get problems with glare. Glare is a special problem for the visually handicapped, and so we've found an off-white paper. Of course, we'd never know about these things if the librarians didn't tell us."

Practical materials are also found in large-print library collections—such titles as *Help Yourself to a Job, A Guide to Retirees, Sex After Sixty, Living with Your Eye Operation.* Tape cassettes and large-print manuals put out by The Center for Independent Living are designed to train newly blind individuals, many of whom are elderly, in housekeeping skills, mobility, and in daily living activities.

Many local libraries produce their own large-print materials as they see a need. The Monroe County (New York) Public Library is printing a large-print directory of department stores. The Oklahoma Department of Libraries produces a large-print weekly newspaper column written at the fourth-grade reading level but geared to adult interests. The column is offered free to the state's 228 newspapers and carries world and national, but mostly Oklahoma, news.

The primary problem with large-print materials is that there simply is not enough of them. The demand far exceeds their production.

Talking Books and Service to the Elderly Handicapped

Robert Frost reading his own poetry; William F. Buckley reading his spy novel, *Saving the Queen;* Alistair Cooke reading *Alistair Cooke's America;* Perry Thomas reading *Down These Mean Streets;* Pearl Bailey reading her own cookbook, *Pearl's Kitchen*—these are but a few of the "talking books" produced on records and cassette tapes by the Division of the Blind and Physically Handicapped of the Library of Congress. Library of Congress talking books and books in Braille are available to anyone who cannot read ordinary print, either because of visual impairment or a physical handicap that prevents them from being able to handle a book, such as the inability to turn a page or to sit up in bed. An estimated 60 per cent of the persons served by this program are over sixty.

The service was begun in 1931 with passage of the Pratt-Smoot Bill which allotted $100,000 to the Library of Congress to provide books for blind adults. Congress has since expanded service to include children (1952), the physically handicapped (1966), and additional materials such as musical scores, instructional texts, and other specialized materials (1962). The program now has an annual budget in excess of $28 million.

The Library of Congress also supplies special playback machines for the individual user. These are required because the tapes and records are produced at lower than commercial speeds. This allows much more to be packed onto an inch of tape or disc and protects the interests of commercial publishers, who receive no payment from the Library of Congress for copyright use. In addition to the talking books, which range from the Bible through classics to current best sellers, magazines such as *American Heritage, Ebony, Newsweek,* and *Retirement Living* are available on flexible discs which can be thrown away after use. Professional magazines such as *Foreign Affairs, The Writer,* and the *Journal of Social Work* are available on tape cassettes which are loaned and returned. Highly practical information is also to be had on records; for example, information about Social Security disability benefits for blind people, Supplemental Security Income for the Aged, Medicare, as well as books and pamphlets on home improvement, cooking, gardening, child care, personal finance, and consumer protection. The playback machines used by the readers are maintained on a voluntary basis by a national organization of telephone employees, who donate their off hours to the service.

The more than 576,000 readers who use these special materials receive them through a network of 56 regional and 102 subregional libraries. In most states there is only one Library for the Blind and Physically Handicapped—this is usually the state library. People are expected to write or telephone for the tapes, records, or Braille books they wish to have mailed to them. Distribution and storage of these materials is not paid for by Congress; the cost must be borne by the state or local library agency.

The Library of Congress estimates that as many as seven million people eligible to receive talking books are not now being reached.

Additional handicapped people could be reached through local, personalized library service. Insufficient local funds has made this difficult, but where it has been tried results have been impressive. When the Great River (Illinois) Library System became a subregional library in the spring of 1973, approximately eighty-five handicapped users were being served with materials for the blind. Two years later, the number had reached over five hundred, an increase of 588 per cent.

Many of the elderly blind and handicapped live alone and find the equipment and mechanics of the service confusing. The need to help elderly inner-city residents know about and use talking books prompted the Enoch Pratt Free Library in Baltimore to assign community aides to visit potential users, first to introduce the service and reassure people that it was free, then to deliver the player and explain how it worked, and then to help with the selection of materials. A strong outreach program has also been developed by the District of Columbia's Regional Library for the Blind and Physically Handicapped. "We have found a number of eligible older readers in large housing developments, people suffering from diabetes or poor health care," reports Grace Lyons, the regional librarian. "These people have a lot of leisure time talking books can fill, and they enjoy the service once it is introduced." In rural Arizona new readers are reached by a special bookmobile operated by the Desert Regional Library and the Easter Seal Society.

The Library of Congress program is able to produce only twelve hundred book titles each year and seventy of the more than nine thousand periodicals that are regularly published. Some public libraries offer radio reading in an effort to provide a more complete library service to the blind and physically handicapped. This service is an excellent answer to the needs of blind persons with arthritic hands or other restrictions on their mobility. The Seattle Radio Talking Book program of the Washington Regional Library for the Blind and Physically Handicapped broadcasts both the morning and evening newspapers at the same time they are being read by the public at large. The Seattle library also devotes entire programs to magazine articles on science, animals, the environment, gardening, home decorating, and other topics chosen by a consumers' program committee. (Any listener is welcome to become a member of the committee and volunteers are extensively used by the Washington Regional Library in providing this service.) These programs provide in-depth coverage of events unavailable on television or radio news programs. One of the most popular radio reading programs in Seattle is "Food Facts," which provides an impartial reading of grocery ads and best buys of the week. This is supplemented by a program which emphasizes meals that can be prepared from the special items advertised by local food stores. And, of course, histories, biographies, and guidebooks of regional interest are also read over the Seattle Radio Talking Book.

Radio reading is a new outreach service for libraries. By the end of 1977, libraries in Erie, Lancaster, and York, Pennsylvania; in Nashville, Tennessee; in Jamestown, New York; and Salt Lake City, Utah; as well as Seattle were providing this service. "They have been reaching many of the elderly blind and handicapped who had never before been linked to social services of any kind," says John Movihill of the American Foundation for the Blind. "Libraries have also found that radio reading services have increased the use of their libraries, too."

Service to Shut-ins

"Call Me," say the words written at the top of the flyer. "I want to visit those of you who cannot visit me. If you are unable to come in to the Scranton Public Library, I would enjoy bringing the Library's Services to you. . . ."

Flyers are brought to homebound older adults by nurses from the Visiting Nurses Association, on trays delivered by Meals on Wheels, and by other social workers who visit the elderly. Batches of flyers are mailed to each of the local social-service agencies which deal with the elderly. They are displayed on bulletin boards in lobbies and recreation rooms of housing units for the elderly, in nutrition centers, in senior citizen centers, in churches and synagogues.

Librarians have long recognized the need to provide service to homebound elderly. The challenge has been learning how to reach them. In 1967, when the Milwaukee Public Library began its "Over 60" service, a team of community aides went pounding on doors. "We tried to work with church groups but found that they were reluctant to give us names," explains Doris Roy Nix, librarian in charge. "So we just went door to door in the older parts of the city where we thought there were a lot of older people. If we didn't find shut-ins ourselves, we often found those who could steer us to friends and relatives who were shut in in other parts of the city. . . . And gradually that was how we built up our shut-in clientele." The service is so well known now that the visiting nurse and health agencies automatically refer patients to the library's shut-in service. Eligible candidates who are unable to travel to a bookmobile or branch library are interviewed in person by a librarian to learn about the kinds of materials the person would like to receive. Each shut-in, on a regular basis, deals with the same librarian whose job is to become familiar with the client's interests and to select appropriate materials.

The demands of the frail lady confined to a wheelchair who wants "more mysteries, the bloodier the better" are relatively simple to meet. More difficult are the requests of an eighty-one-year-old former symphony orchestra violinist for "specific concerti, symphonies, and other classical recordings as played by specific symphony orchestras." Explains the Milwaukee librarian who works with him, "Although fulfilling his desires takes a considerable amount of time, his enjoyment of all the materials he receives makes it well worthwhile."

Books and materials are delivered to the door of each shut-in about every three weeks. A maximum of twenty books are delivered at a time. "That's about the limit," says Mrs. Nix, "because we pack them into bags and the person who carries the bags can carry two of them." Deliveries are made by community aides who are themselves retired people. "We try to send the same aide to the same shut-in so that there is a certain amount of personal contact involved . . . sometimes friendships spring up." The community aides currently range in age from sixty-four to seventy-six. They are recruited by the Milwaukee City Service Commission, work twelve hours a week, and in addition to their hourly wage, are reimbursed for travel expenses. The library requires that aides know something about books, but the primary consideration is that they like to work with people, are friendly, and skillful in encouraging reading. Milwaukee finds that the aides are able to dispel the suspicion and hostility which often characterizes elderly shut-ins.

Volunteers are used by many public libraries to provide personal, individualized service to shut-ins. In Kenosha, Wisconsin, the public library has trained volunteers to read aloud at a center for the elderly. The Los Angeles Public Library has close to 250 volunteers working out of most of the 61 branches and the Central Library to circulate more than 5,700 books, cassettes, records, magazines, music scores, and other materials each month. Dallas' volunteers run the gamut from a television actor to a retired registered nurse, to a seventy-five-year-old man who just completed a bachelor's degree in psychology and who also does volunteer work at the Mental Health Association.

At the Musser Public Library in Muscatine, Iowa, an hour's visit goes along with the fortnightly book delivery service, and the library makes a diligent effort to match volunteers with prospective clients according to reading interests and hobbies.

Rowan Public Library in Salisbury, North Carolina, is proud that their outreach library service to the homebound sometimes enables them to help their clients link up to social services they need. The library recently arranged for housekeeping services through the Council on Aging for an elderly client living alone in one room who had grown increasingly blind.

A simple and inexpensive outreach program to serve homebound people is run by the Cranston (Rhode Island) Public Library. A part-time librarian telephones elderly people served by Meals on Wheels and arranges for the volunteer drivers to deliver library materials to fill the shut-ins' wants.

Special Materials for the Homebound

What kinds of materials do libraries lend their shut-in clients? In addition to books and records, libraries deliver such things as pattern books for crocheting or for making stuffed toys; special games and playing cards for the visually handicapped; cassette players and tapes of old-time hit songs, of radio programs of the thirties and forties such as Jack Benny, Fred Allen, Charlie McCarthy. In some communities, volunteers record church services and school and civic events on cassette tapes for loan to shut-ins. Special equipment is often provided—ceiling projectors for bedridden patients, lighted magnified lenses, special stands to hold books. For Clarence Wraight of Spencer, North Carolina, who has no use of his arms or legs, the Rowan Public Library lends one of its automatic page turners which Mr. Wraight can operate by touching a lever with his chin.

Libraries usually do not charge fines to homebound users nor do they hold them responsible for lost or damaged books. But the question rarely comes up. Elderly people, they find, are very responsible when it comes to protecting library materials. They have learned to appreciate their value.

Nursing Homes and Hospitals

"Books help us to know the patients better," recently observed an administrator of a nursing home in Rhode Island, "and we notice that books help the patients communicate with each other as they swap them back and forth and talk to each other about them." A million persons over sixty-five are presently in institutions in the United States, primarily nursing homes. The number has been rising as the proportion of widowed females in the elderly population has increased.

In Milwaukee, which prides itself on the breadth of its service to the elderly, an "Over 60" Bookmobile makes regular stops in Milwaukee County at large nursing homes (a van serves smaller institutions), homes for the aged, day centers, housing projects, and neighborhoods where many people over sixty live. The Bookmobile is a mini-library carrying some four thousand books to serve a wide variety of interests, as well as large-print books and foreign-language materials. The Bookmobile makes about fifty stops over a three-week schedule, each one lasting about forty-five minutes. It is equipped with a hydraulic lift at the rear which is used for delivering loaded book carts to the nursing homes and for lifting aboard wheelchair patrons who wish to visit the Bookmobile itself.

Wherever this type of institutional service is offered, librarians have discovered that success depends on warm personal contacts made on a regular basis. Much depends on the interest and enthusiasm of the nursing-home staffs, particularly the head of the home. The Monroe County (New York) Public Library finds it helpful to bring nursing-home personnel into the library to familiarize them with the resources which can help them in their professional work—the most current literature in the field of gerontology and nursing care, for example—and materials that can be adapted in imaginative ways for use by their patients.

The librarian in charge of nursing-home service in Skokie, Illinois, says that "an enthusiastic, aware occupational therapist is the connecting link which makes our service work." An art therapist planned a Bicentennial program for residents on the subject of American painters, using framed prints, posters, films, and slides as well as books—all from the Skokie Public Library. Observes another experienced librarian: "Librarians must be prepared to go beyond the basic duty of supplying books. It is difficult to draw a dividing line between giving a library service and acting as a welfare visitor."

What difference does it make to the person being helped? Mollie Shapiro, a sixty-year-old quadriplegic, has been a patient in the Beth Abraham Hospital in the Bronx, New York, for fifteen years. She receives no family visits. She is not only wheelchair-bound, but cannot even lift a finger to turn a page. A few years ago Mrs. Shapiro wrote the following essay in the *Wilson Library Journal* about the pleasure she got from her library books:

> I can visit a distant land, where it takes but a moment to get to, taking in its beauties and meeting its people. These people become my friends as I follow their lives, and I am privileged to share their thoughts and feelings. I know their joys and sufferings. I go on meeting new people all the time, am never bored, and can't wait to see what is going to happen as the story unfolds and to visit the picturesque places with them.
>
> I am never alone and can choose any part of the world I want to, or I can stay in my own neighborhood. I am able to unravel the threads of history, or marvel at the new world of tomorrow. Sometimes I cringe with the victims of war and other times I enjoy the peaceful existence of life on a quiet farm. I may even join a great, rollicking party, without even having to dress up, and go as I am—to join the festivities or stay looking on—no one objects.

CHAPTER 9 ✳✳✳✳✳✳✳✳✳✳✳✳✳✳✳✳✳✳✳✳✳✳✳✳✳✳✳✳✳✳✳✳✳✳✳✳

Fighting for Public Libraries

The mission of the public library is to serve the public.

Not *some* of the public.

All of the public.

Unlike the subscription library of Franklin's day, when the mission of the library was to provide books for a literate few who cared enough to pay hard cash to satisfy their reading appetites, public libraries today exist in a mixed society where most citizens are able to read and write, where their interests vary widely, and where, for some, access to various types of recorded information and the ability to understand that information is essential to their well-being and even their existence in a complicated, technological, government-oriented mode of life.

With the advent of the mass paperback book, the public library has ceased to serve as a primary source of adult "light reading." Increasingly, the public library has become the community's encyclopedia of hard facts about everything under the sun, a reference library for student and adult researchers, a children's reading room, young adults' library, adult-education facility, senior citizens' second home. On top of this, as the community requires it, the public library also serves as information and referral center for social services, job opportunity and career development resource, focal point for programs to reach the poor and undereducated, library service center for institutions, and special library for the blind and handicapped.

These departures from simply serving as a reading shelf for a select group of book users are all to the good. Public tax moneys spent on public libraries should not be used to benefit the select few. There is an affirmative duty for public libraries to serve the entire community, and that means everyone who can use their service to advantage. This is not a process of self-selection, where the librarian can wait behind the counter for knowledgeable users to appear. It includes an obligation on library trustees and staff to determine just what the community's information and reference needs are, to equip the library to serve those needs with materials and qualified personnel, and then to work out effective delivery procedures to get those services to the members of the community who need them.

For many years, one of the basic mistakes public-library administrators have made is to attempt to measure the value of their services in terms of "circulation" and "numbers of users," as if they were running a grocery store. Slowly we have come to realize that a library is not a profit-making business whose success or failure depends on turnover of inventory. It is an *essential community resource* like the hospital and fire department. Eighty-eight per cent of all Americans give the public library top billing as the number-one cultural resource they want in their own community. That is not because they want to go into the library every day and take out a book. Like the hospital and fire station, most people in the community want a public library available so it is there when they need it. One does not measure the success or failure of a hospital by the number of people who become sick or need an operation, or of a fire department by the number of homes or businesses that have conflagrations. It is the size of the community served, the number of people in the general population, which is the proper measure of the need for a public library and the size of its staff and budget.

Where measurement of library users becomes important is in the field of special library services necessitated because of the special characteristics of the community the library serves. It *is* significant for supplemental budget allocations to know how many disadvantaged users are given special literacy training or social-service counseling in a public library located in a low-income community; or how many blind or institutional users are served by a public library in a community with an especially high proportion of senior citizens. Here the numbers provide a measurement of the effectiveness of special programs and an indication of additional funding requirements.

Every public library should be sufficiently funded in regular annual governmental budget allotments to provide an adequate level of library service to all segments of the general population within the library's area of service: young children, older students, adult researchers, senior citizens, and those of all ages who seek advancement or self-education. The logical way to do this is on a straight per capita of population budget allocation.

Special government grants should also be provided for special user services in those communities where the need for special services exists and extra staff and materials are required (e.g., job counseling, literacy training, prison library services). These grants should be sufficient for the costs of the necessary additional materials, technology, and hiring and training of personnel to permit affirmative library action programs to reach and help those citizens who need such services.

We do not have a system of public-library financing today which permits such operations. A few communities and states may have approached that result, but it has been largely by chance. This has partly been because the role of public libraries has been going through a period of evolution, just as our society has been going through the evolution of higher levels of compulsory education, availability of radio and television sets in every home, the explosion in magazines, comic books, and mass paperbacks. These have all had an impact on the public's need for libraries and new types of library services.

The other reason for the absence of a rational, uniform approach to public-library funding has been the failure of legislators and budget directors to recognize the need for basic library services measured on a population basis.

Happily, a number of farsighted library trustees, library administrators, and individual librarians have recognized the shifting needs for public-library services and have met the challenge despite the lack of proper funding. Special demonstration grants, the majority made possible with federal funds, have also permitted the development of many worthwhile pilot programs to meet special user needs.

The point is that the period of hit-or-miss planning should be behind us. We know now what basic services public libraries should be providing today, and we know that special services can help meet the special needs in most communities. The time has come to put these lessons into use. In short, the time has come to bring about a national program of public-library funding that will assure fair access to public-library service on an equal basis to all Americans.

GETTING INTO THE FIGHT

As this is being written, preparations are under way for the White House Conference on Libraries and Information Science scheduled to be held in Washington, D.C., in September 1979. Various state conferences have been or are being held in preparation for the White House Conference. Most observers believe that the conference will be a major opportunity for establishing national policies for library operations. And well it may.

But the thing for citizens concerned with public libraries to keep in mind is that the White House Conference will cover the library waterfront, so to speak. It will include school libraries, college libraries, research libraries, medical libraries, and special libraries, in addition to whatever attention can be given to public libraries. It will also cover such questions as the establishment of a national library, a national library network, interlibrary cooperation, state library agencies, personnel training, and new technologies. There will be participants with their own special concerns, including book publishers, computer manufacturers, library equipment dealers, and others with profit interest to protect.

Who will be speaking up for the public library?

That is where we come in, dear reader. Our job as library users is to be sure that the public library receives its fair share of attention and consideration; that the proper role of the public library is understood; and that any national library program includes the concept of public funding on a per capita basis of public-library services throughout the country.

What form should that funding take? The National Commission on Libraries and Information Science recommended in 1974 a federal-state-local matching grant formula. That is an approach which has worked well in other contexts of governmental aid and there is no reason why it should not work well here. The details of the formula can be left to the legislative experts; the important thing is the principle—spreading the base of public financial support to eliminate uncertainty in public-library planning, and at the same time to give recognition to the national and state interests which are being served by public libraries on the community level.

The logical vehicle for any national program of public library funding would be a new "National Library Act" to encompass all of the national programs developed as a result of the White House Conference. Public-library funding must be included in any such legislation.

One other feature of a new national library program that will be of interest to public libraries, of course, is the development of delivery services to permit data on federal health programs, for example, to be available to a small community public library immediately on demand whenever a request comes in from an individual library user with a health-service need. Similar delivery services should be available on such varied topics as employment openings in different parts of the country; the status of pending congressional legislation; FDA safety information on new products; governmental bibliographies on space technology; current U.S. State Department information about conditions in a foreign country; or any other type of government-related information. A computer terminal in every public library with access to such a range of information from a central source, possibly combined with facsimile transmission capability, is the type of advance in information science we should support and applaud.

But the main issue is still the ability to deliver library services to the individual library user in the individual local public library. And that in turn requires a new federal-state partnership in providing per capita library aid, supplemented by special grants for special user services.

It would be a serious mistake to sit back and assume that common sense will win out on its own accord, and that the White House Conference will automatically adopt enlightened public library policies.

One must recognize that the subjects that will receive attention at the White House Conference will be those prescribed by its organizers. The competition for attention to particular topics and issues could well result in a shortchanging of public libraries.

White House conferences do not enact laws; they only produce recommendations, and often those recommendations are disregarded or quickly forgotten.

For that reason alone, it is critical for concerned citizens who are willing to fight for public libraries to carry the fight to where it will do the most good.

1. *The President.* Jimmy Carter made a campaign pledge to aid the nation's libraries. He should be reminded of the needs of public libraries again and again, at every opportunity.

2. *Congress.* The key to any national program to aid public libraries and establish the principle of per capita library aid plus special grants for special user services is the United States Congress. Two steps are involved: Enacting authorizing legislation to describe what the program is; and appropriating the funds to make the program work. Already Congress has demonstrated under LSCA how it can authorize funds for library services and then not appropriate the money to do the job. The key congressmen for public-library-funding programs are the members of these committees:

Authorizing legislation:

Senate Committee on Human Resources (Education, Arts, and Humanities Subcommittee)

House Committee on Education and Labor (Select Education Sub-committee)

Appropriation of funds:

Senate Committee on Appropriations (Labor, HEW Subcommittee)

House Committee on Appropriations (Labor, HEW Subcommittee)

Of course, the members of these committees listen to their colleagues, so the place for any citizen to begin in fighting for public libraries is with his or her own congressman and U.S. senator.

3. *State Government.* There are three critical points in each state for obtaining aid for public libraries: (a) the governor, who initiates the budget for the expenditure of state tax revenues, including matching funds; (b) the state library agency, which should develop the program and standards for financial aid to public libraries; and (c) the state legislature, which votes on the governor's budget, proposes its own additions, and appropriates the money to carry out the budget. Here the same principle of beginning the fight for public libraries with one's own legislative representatives is the right way to get started.

4. *Local Government.* Here is where the greatest variety in funding procedures exists, and citizens should familiarize themselves with the key personnel and procedures for ensuring that public libraries hold their own in the competition for local funds.

5. *News Media.* Elected public officials read the newspapers every single day, looking for mention of their name. When they are praised by citizen groups, they are pleased. When they are criticized, they wince. When they are urged to take action, they normally respond. Citizens fighting for public libraries should enlist their local newspaper, radio, and television stations in the fight. They will be strong and useful allies.

6. *The Library Board and Staff.* The ultimate object of the fight for public libraries, the library representatives, should also be involved from the start, as informed observers if nothing else. Li-

brary trustees are usually citizens with "clout" and they can often help with legislators, congressmen, and other officials. Library administrators should be good sources of ammunition for arguments based on local needs, and should also be aware of what will be expected of them when the fight succeeds.

There has never been a better time or a greater opportunity to transform America's public libraries into community library service centers for all her people. Citizens who are willing to join the fight for public libraries have a very special opportunity to participate in a worthy cause at exactly the right moment.

The fight is a good one.

The cause is just.

Victory will make a major contribution to the nation's future.

APPENDIXES

APPENDIX A

Mission Statement for Public Libraries

*The Board of Directors of the Public Library Association adopted
the following draft statement at the 1977 American Library Association Annual Conference. When completed, these guidelines will serve
as the library profession's guide to public library development until
new principles are formally adopted in the mid-1980s. A section
dealing with background has been omitted.*

The nation's public libraries are in serious trouble. For the most
part, the public library of today is still geared to the social needs of the
19th century which created it. It is the intent of the mission statement
to show that the needs of society at the close of the 20th century
demand that the public library change and that the public library assume a strong leadership role. The focus of the mission statement is on
the output of the public library—user-oriented services which meet
certain needs of citizens and society as only the public library can
meet them.

Societal Change

In its 19th-century beginnings the American public library was an
agency structured to respond to certain basic societal needs. In the
20th century, changes have occurred in society which suggest altered
views of the mission of the public library and correspondingly in the
structure of its services. Although the mission of the public library
today has its roots in the society of the past, the milieu in which the
public library now functions demands shifts of emphasis radical in degree if not in kind. Among these new factors in American society demanding a new institution are:

1) *Runaway Social Change*

By virtue of new forms of communication, undreamed of in previous revolutionary periods, nearly everyone is simultaneously present at all major events, as aired, for example, on the 6 o'clock TV news. The natural tendency of revolution to destroy the old order *before* building a new one is now no longer restrained. Society is thus in genuine danger of destroying the positive insights, attitudes, and values of the past before they can be assimilated into a more civilized new order.

Society needs an agency to operate, as it were, in the eye of the revolutionary storm, to keep the radical new thrust in some continuity with the past and to help preserve and bridge the future. Society needs an agency to preserve and make widely accessible the record of past human experience—to stimulate thoughtful people everywhere to discern positive insights and values from the past and to assimilate them into the new order. The mass media—press, TV, radio, etc.—by their very nature tend to concentrate on the current scene rather than on the past.

Because change now occurs so rapidly, the majority of individuals and institutions today suffer future shock—a sense of alienation from the world and from themselves, a sense of powerlessness in coping with, let alone controlling, the direction of life. To enable individuals and institutions to cope with future shock, society needs an agency to identify relationships in the fast-flowing river of change and to maintain the record of new ideas, technologies, and values, so that individuals and institutions will be able to perceive and then control the direction of change as it relates to each person's particular life experience.

2) *Exponential Increase in the Volume and Complexity of the Record of Human Experience*

Perhaps for the first time in history, barriers to the human record exist not so much in a scarcity of material as in a glut. Unprecedented increases in the record, stemming partly from the knowledge explosion itself and partly from the capacity of technology to record and preserve *everything* in a multiplicity of forms (print, nonprint, and electronic), have resulted in a growing mass of trivial and redundant material which threatens to engulf the information seeker. This occurs at a time when the need for authentic information is greater than ever.

As a consequence of this information overload, the role of libraries for several thousand years, which emphasizes the preservation of the human record, has now become more complex, requiring hard decisions not only about what is to be preserved but also about what is to be discarded. Decisions are, and must be, made to erase portions of the record deemed to be insignificant, irrelevant, and unrepresentative, in order that the useful and pertinent be accessible.

Although the process of erasing no longer needed data has been commonplace in today's society (for example, large data banks supporting daily editions of newspapers are erased regularly), there is as yet no agency accountable to the community as a whole accepting this responsibility. Most decisions to erase information are made today at the local and typically at the institution level. If, however, information is to be erased, lost for all time, then society needs as democratic a process as possible to diffuse this responsibility and involve as many people as possible in determining which data is to be preserved and which data is to be erased.

Society needs an agency to guide the user at all levels to the most significant representative materials to meet each individual's need for information, knowledge, and ideas. In order to meet those needs, society needs an agency to digest, evaluate, and make responsible decisions to retain or to erase the materials produced. Society needs an agency with accountability to the whole community to assume leadership in coordinating the numerous agencies and institutions which generate, preserve, and disseminate the current record of experience. Society needs an agency to maintain certain portions of the record and to develop effective networks capable of supplying the record when and where it is needed.

3) *Total Egalitarianism*

For the first time in history, the concept of the *right* of every individual to determine her or his own destiny, and the *obligation* of every individual to contribute to social decision is now becoming operative. Correlative to our practical acceptance of the equality of all citizens is the need of all people for access to the record of human experience, both past and present. Society needs an agency that can actively bring every person, regardless of age, education, language, religion, ethnic and cultural background, and mental and physical health, into effective contact with the human record.

4) *Depletion of Natural Resources*

For the first time in American history, the possibility, indeed the probability, is becoming generally recognized that natural resources, especially energy resources, are not unlimited and that these resources may be eroded or even exhausted in the foreseeable future. Society is also becoming aware of how we have over-used and misused the environment and thus are in danger of destroying the possibility of life on this planet, let alone its quality.

This situation, now recognized throughout society, is probably the death knell to American frontier isolationism mentality because problems of ecology and energy are clearly global and underscore the interdependence of all nations. The situation signals the end of the American dream of unlimited expansion, unlimited power, and unlimited mobility. It signals a rethinking of what underlies our concepts of the "good life":—a reexamination of national, institutional, and individual priorities.

It is possible that the danger in which society now finds itself will be the catalyst for a flowering of scientific and humanistic creativity: the discovery of new sources of energy and new technologies to restore and improve the environment.

In the face of a world which may be vastly altered, society needs an agency to help people to be realistic, to plan rather than to panic. Society needs an agency to help people keep abreast of the ecological facts as they develop, to separate ecological truth from the accelerating currents of propaganda and special interests, and to draw upon the wisdom of past experience as we reassess our values and options, both individual and social.

These four factors in society as it is today—Runaway Social Change, Exponential Increase in the Volume and Complexity of the Record of Human Experience, Total Egalitarianism, and Depletion of Natural Resources—suggest a new focus for the *mission* of the public library, with correlative shifts in its governance and administration, its delivery structure, its materials (in both content and form), its personnel and required competencies, its services, and its relationships to other libraries and allied cultural, educational, social, and informational agencies.

The public library meets broad social needs, but its characteristic mode of operation is individualized whether the user is a person, a group, an organization, a business, or a government. It is therefore essential that the public library focus not only on major social trends but also on techniques to identify and meet unique individual needs.

Needed Responses

If one were to invent an information agency to respond to the social needs of today, that new agency would need to perform the following services:

1) Provide access to the human records of the past—factual, imaginative, scientific, and humanistic—partly through its own collections and partly through an effective network linking all collections in the region, state, nation, and the world.

2) Organize this human record so that access can be made to it from a myriad of directions allowing not only the facts but also the wisdom in the record to be retrieved. The agency would facilitate cross connections within the record, among many disciplines, many literary forms, many periods of history.

3) Collect, translate, and organize the human record on all intellectual levels in many packages, print and nonprint.

4) Conduct a vigorous program of dissemination dramatizing the relevance of the record of past and present human experience to resolving today's problems. The program would include public information about what is available, guidance to individuals in its use, and group activities designed to foster interpersonal dialogue.

5) Develop, in cooperation with other information agencies and libraries, a responsible policy for preserving and erasing portions of humankind's voluminous current record as described in the section dealing with the Exponential Increase in the Volume and Complexity of the Record of Human Experience. It would negotiate consensus about criteria for judging between materials which are significant or representative and those which are trivial or redundant.

6) Take leadership in defining a new statement of professional ethics and in creating new structures to protect intellectual freedom in the light of the responsibility to preserve or erase.

7) Take a leadership role in coordinating the acquisition policies of other libraries and information agencies, because no one agency can

be expected to preserve all significant and representative materials in all forms at all levels.

8) Having developed policies for shared acquisition, assume leadership in creating and maintaining an effective network so that all citizens would have easy access to any record, no matter where it was stored.

9) Not only select, collect, organize, and preserve the human record, but become expert in using flexible procedures for allowing citizens to inform themselves uniquely.

10) Package and present the human record to allow easy access for people previously excluded by lack of education, lack of language facility, ethnic or cultural backgrounds, age, physical or mental handicaps, and apathy.

To accomplish all of the above, the agency would need to be accountable to the *total* community, rather than to some specific segment or constituency. It would need to be a *public* agency, publicly supported and publicly controlled, because its responsibilities would be of central social importance. It would need to be a *flexible* agency, able to respond to as yet undefined social needs which may emerge in a changing world.

The agency described in the proceeding ten categories does not yet exist. The awesome responsibilities described could not, and should not, be vested in only one type of library, or indeed in librarianship alone. Nevertheless, libraries in general are the agency to which American society has assigned primary responsibility to identify, select, organize, retrieve, disseminate, and make totally accessible the record of human thought. Libraries collectively must be the agency described above.

The specific role of the public library in responding to the broad needs of society grows out of its existence as a public agency, with broad tax support and the responsibility to serve the total community rather than a specific clientele. For the user with specialized information needs, the public library must continue to act as a point of entry into the national network of libraries and information resources. For individuals or groups in their other life roles, the public library must continue to act as a popularizer, making the human record accessible, alerting people to it and stimulating its use. As the one type of library accountable to the total community, the public library of the future must play a strong coordinative role, leading all libraries in their response to today's new social needs.

Summary Statement

This document describes nothing that is entirely new. Some public libraries across the nation are already attempting to respond to these new demands. In aggregate, their efforts anticipate the public library of the 21st century.

The unique characteristics of the public library are in its very generalness and in its role of popularizer. The public library considers the entire spectrum of knowledge to be its purview, and it considers the entire spectrum of the community as its user population. Further, the public library is particularly sensitive to the information needs and flows in the community; its funding base is that of the total community; and it is unfettered by the impingements of a parental organization. The very closeness of the public library to total community priorities is a source of its strength. Another source of public library strength is its unique mode of operation, which is individualized.

It is only through links with other more specialized libraries and information agencies that the totality of the public library mission can be accomplished. The public library assumes leadership responsibility with the state library and other regional and national organizations for linking community resources to other resources in the state, nation, and world.

Upon completion of the Public Library Association's research project to create a process of standards development, professional leaders should have the tools to construct new and even radically different standards. The research should pave the way for the kinds of standards which will speed the necessary shift from institution- and input-oriented evaluation to output- and user-oriented evaluation. The Public Library Association intends this document to be useful to librarians and community leaders not only as an interim statement but as a bridge to the new and long desired approach to library standards. This statement is the charge by the Public Library Association to lay and professional leaders for the delivery of library services in the last quarter of the 20th century.

APPENDIX B

TABLE I
GOVERNMENT FUNDING OF PUBLIC LIBRARIES
Percentage Government Shares of the Cost of
Operating Public Libraries

State	Total Public Libraries (including Branches)	Government Funding of Public Libraries, 1975 (in millions)	Federal Share	State Share	Local Share
Alabama	199	$ 9.33	16.7%	8.9%	74.4%
Alaska	39	2.0*	18.8	25.8	55.4
Arizona	97	7.1*	9.5	6.7	83.8
Arkansas	171	5.52	18.2	15.5	66.3
California	977	165.36	2.4	2.1	95.5
Colorado	181	15.86	11.3	.6	88.1
Connecticut	258	16.0*	5.5	12.3	82.1
Delaware	25	1.5*	22.2	4.3	73.5
Florida	277	17.0*	7.2	7.5	85.3
Georgia	275	19.34	7.3	36.9	55.8
Hawaii	40	5.58	6.7	93.3	0
Idaho	86	3.74	17.8	12.5	69.7
Illinois	656	72.51	4.9	18.5	76.6
Indiana	358	29.20	2.6	2.9	94.5
Iowa	528	13.06	8.6	3.8	87.6
Kansas	354	5.8*	13.1	7.0	79.9
Kentucky	174	15.35	10.1	36.3	53.6
Louisiana	279	14.68	7.4	4.2	88.4
Maine	225	5.50	11.1	20.1	68.8
Maryland	157	32.96	5.0	16.6	78.4
Massachusetts	563	47.72	1.9	11.1	87.0
Michigan	579	53.18	4.8	10.8	84.4
Minnesota	301	22.01	3.7	10.0	86.3
Mississippi	232	8.15	13.3	19.2	67.5
Missouri	335	17.81	9.4	7.0	83.6

State	Total Public Libraries (including Branches)	Government Funding of Public Libraries, 1975 (in millions)	Federal Share	State Share	Local Share
Montana	99	3.16	17.3	5.8	76.9
Nebraska	282	6.72	7.1	18.1	74.8
Nevada	45	2.64	9.0	21.8	69.2
New Hampshire	216	3.2*	17.4	15.5	67.1
New Jersey	468	53.45	2.9	21.7	75.4
New Mexico	51	4.43	10.4	16.0	73.6
New York	1085	176.25	2.1	17.1	80.8
North Carolina	172	18.82	10.6	25.2	64.2
North Dakota	71	2.32	27.1	8.3	64.6
Ohio	651	67.25	4.1	3.7	92.2
Oklahoma	165	7.8*	13.4	10.9	75.7
Oregon	171	10.44	6.2	7.1	86.7
Pennsylvania	562	42.97	6.6	23.2	70.2
Rhode Island	81	5.96	10.1	18.6	71.3
South Carolina	127	6.49	9.7	24.1	66.2
South Dakota	95	2.60	14.5	12.4	73.1
Tennessee	234	12.68	9.2	15.3	77.5
Texas	519	35.84	12.5	3.9	83.6
Utah	78	7.57	7.7	14.2	78.1
Vermont	181	1.5*	30.5	29.9	39.6
Virginia	186	26.46	3.9	11.3	84.8
Washington	276	28.33	4.3	11.4	84.3
West Virginia	92	4.2*	17.7	13.9	68.5
Wisconsin	402	31.10	3.7	12.0	84.3
Wyoming	73	3.26	12.9	17.6	69.5

Sources: Number of public libraries in each state from R. R. Bowker & Co. unpublished list as of September 1976. Other data from report prepared for the National Commission on Public Libraries and Information Science by Government Studies & Systems, Philadelphia (October 1976).
* 1972 figures from National Commission on Libraries and Information Service, "Alternatives for Financing the Public Library" (May 1974).

TABLE II
Comparison of Per Student Allocations of Funds to
Campus and Public Libraries

State	Total Students*	Total Tax Dollar Funding of Colleges and Universities (per student)	Expenditures for Campus Libraries (per student)	Expenditures for Public Libraries (per student)
Alabama	117,081	$2,178.00	$106.00	$2.43
Alaska	7,653	7,452.00	324.00	8.12
Arizona	113,692	2,059.00	94.00	4.81
Arkansas	47,891	2,472.00	130.00	2.06
California	1,049,616	2,979.00	111.00	7.81
Colorado	114,622	2,197.00	102.00	6.26
Connecticut	109,648	1,952.00	194.00	7.88
Delaware	20,021	2,243.00	149.00	2.63
Florida	227,462	2,425.00	128.00	3.49
Georgia	131,676	2,392.00	156.00	2.52
Hawaii	35,595	3,033.00	131.00	8.17
Idaho	29,181	2,161.00	135.00	3.69
Illinois	390,936	2,541.00	136.00	5.70
Indiana	165,354	2,016.00	134.00	5.21
Iowa	101,540	2,461.00	141.00	4.45
Kansas	91,444	2,179.00	112.00	3.21
Kentucky	92,193	2,596.00	132.00	3.90
Louisiana	118,524	2,085.00	110.00	3.86
Maine	31,882	1,796.00	129.00	3.45
Maryland	136,490	3,532.00	169.00	8.26
Massachusetts	286,288	1,887.00	173.00	9.57
Michigan	334,567	2,182.00	120.00	4.12
Minnesota	137,123	2,221.00	134.00	6.43
Mississippi	75,275	2,388.00	97.00	3.15
Missouri	159,453	2,051.00	126.00	5.20
Montana	25,035	1,985.00	99.00	5.14
Nebraska	55,315	2,227.00	134.00	5.74
Nevada	19,679	1,773.00	137.00	6.23
New Hampshire	31,103	1,422.00	195.00	5.22
New Jersey	199,215	2,002.00	150.00	6.87

State	Total Students*	Total Tax Dollar Funding of Colleges and Universities (per student)	Expenditures for Campus Libraries (per student)	Expenditures for Public Libraries (per student)
New Mexico	39,548	2,374.00	174.00	5.05
New York	715,740	2,465.00	157.00	7.28
North Carolina	190,859	2,738.00	162.00	3.27
North Dakota	25,622	2,047.00	99.00	3.17
Ohio	328,281	1,603.00	120.00	3.47
Oklahoma	104,386	1,423.00	89.00	3.86
Oregon	105,254	2,111.00	116.00	5.58
Pennsylvania	355,432	1,964.00	98.00	2.78
Rhode Island	43,823	1,459.00	145.00	5.74
South Carolina	91,762	2,409.00	142.00	2.77
South Dakota	23,712	1,920.00	111.00	4.37
Tennessee	138,247	1,973.00	139.00	4.16
Texas	438,151	2,122.00	128.00	3.39
Utah	70,387	1,822.00	82.00	6.37
Vermont	24,424	1,373.00	163.00	4.87
Virginia	158,500	1,825.00	156.00	4.74
Washington	159,567	2,477.00	142.00	7.92
West Virginia	56,809	1,735.00	115.00	3.48
Wisconsin	178,169	2,884.00	131.00	6.38
Wyoming	13,773	2,609.00	111.00	7.41

Sources: College and University library information is for the 1974–75 fiscal year and is based on unpublished data in the National Center for Education Statistics and *Evaluation of the Effectiveness of Federal Funding of Public Libraries,* prepared for the National Commission on Libraries and Information Science by Government Studies and Systems, Inc., Philadelphia, December 1976. Public library data is based on per capita information for 1975 computed from the U.S. Bureau of the Census "State Government Finance in 1975" and from unpublished data in the Governments Division.

* College and University full-time equivalent of total enrollment.

APPENDIX C

President Jimmy Carter on Libraries

(*Excerpts from a campaign statement issued in August 1976*)

Well-stocked libraries open to all are essential to our democratic system of government. As President Kennedy said in 1963, "Good libraries are as essential to an educated and informed people as the school system itself. The library is not only the custodian of our cultural heritage but the key to progress and the advancement of knowledge." . . .

Because of federal cutbacks and local budget stringencies, academic and research libraries have been forced to sharply curtail their acquisition of library materials. Some of the greatest center city public libraries have had to reduce their hours of service, lay off personnel, and eliminate programs. Elementary schools in some cases have closed their libraries altogether, dismissing library personnel and dividing up the books among the classrooms. We cannot call for a revival of quality education in America and close our libraries. We cannot ask our children to learn to read and take away their books.

We need a new, revitalized effort to save our libraries and to make them strong bastions against illiteracy and ignorance.

This is not simply a matter of more federal support, although that will help. In libraries as in other areas, we need efficiency and sound management of our limited resources. We need to organize our library services so that they can effectively serve the public. We need to coordinate federal help for libraries so that the assistance reaches those who need it and so that waste and duplication are eliminated.

Streamlining of government, and coordination between the federal government and the states must be pursued with vigor. At present, federal assistance is uncoordinated, confused, and multifaceted. The U.S. Office of Education administers three library programs designed to assist the states to improve their school libraries, develop their public libraries, and help colleges and universities strengthen their library programs.

The National Science Foundation administers a program of science information activities. The Library of Congress serves as a national library, distributes cataloging data to libraries across the country, makes talking books available to the blind and physically handicapped, and works in a host of different ways to improve the services of all types of libraries in America. The National Library of Medicine supplies up-to-date medical information to health science professionals all over the country.

There are many other federal agencies involved in the nation's library systems. There is the National Commission on Libraries and Information Science, the National Endowment for the Humanities, and the Depository Library program of the Government Printing Office, all involved in one phase or another of library assistance. Grants are available for library construction through the U.S. Office of Education, the U.S. Department of Housing and Urban Development, the U.S. Department of Commerce, and through the Appalachian Regional Commission. The list of library-related federal agencies and services could go on and on.

If federal library help is to be truly useful to the states, to the localities and to library users, we must rationalize and coordinate this disconnected system. We need a clear, ongoing national library policy, coordinated by a well-organized centrally controlled federal agency.

A logical agent for delivery of library support to the nation is a national library. The Library of Congress has been allowed to assume some of these functions. It is possible that it should assume others. As part of my overall effort to reorganize government I intend to study the feasibility of strengthening the role of the Library of Congress in coordinating national library policy.

Along with greater coordination in Washington, we need to strengthen the leadership role of state governments in the provision of library services. The local libraries should be able to look with confidence to the state government, and in turn the state should know what kinds of assistance and advice can be sought from Washington. We will coordinate the myriad federal agencies and programs assisting libraries and draw the lines with simplicity and clarity. The states must do the same, by simplifying and modernizing their own bureaucratic structures. Paperwork and bureaucratic red tape must be eliminated in Washington. In turn, the states must reduce their own bureaucratic complexities and eliminate their own red tape. It is no help to our cities, counties, and towns if the federal paperwork burden is simply replaced by the state paperwork burden. Proper management and a reformed bureaucracy may themselves make more money available for books and direct services to the public.

We must have rationalized library development. The large research libraries should be strengthened so that they can serve not only their primary clientele but also smaller libraries in every state. Major research collections should supplement the more general collections of the smaller libraries. Each library should be coordinated with other libraries in its region, so that it will know where it can turn to borrow a book it does not own. Through coordination of this kind, every American will have access to the library holdings of our greatest research libraries.

Improved research and development are required, so that automated techniques of information retrieval can be applied to libraries. But we must be careful to implement only the most cost-effective and carefully tested systems. It is easy to waste money on sophisticated technology that is unnecessary or inadequate, or that makes the provision of service more difficult or more time-consuming.

If we are to succeed in developing libraries to their full service potential we must have the interest and participation of large numbers of the American public. The President is authorized to hold a White House Conference on Library and Information Services . . . for this purpose.

This conference should be the culmination of an extensive process of citizen involvement in library policy making its beginning at the grassroots. Through preliminary conferences in each of the states, the local citizenry can take a close look at their libraries and decide whether perhaps there are overlapping roles and responsibilities of public libraries, new services needed, or other changes that need to be made.

These are decisions that must be approved at the state and local level by an informed and knowledgeable citizenry. The White House Conference process will help to develop a public knowledgeable about alternative ways of providing good library service, and it will help create public support for libraries. Results from the state conferences can be pooled at the White House Conference. We will then have a sound foundation upon which to devise complementary local, state, and federal plans for library and information services in the decade ahead.

Let me summarize the points I have made. First, I believe that federal help for the nation's library system should be funded on a sustained and stable basis. If we are to have an educated and informed population we need a strong and open library system supported by a committed administration.

Second, I believe that federal library help must be rationalized, consolidated, and streamlined. This process of cutting red tape must be accompanied by a commitment at the state and local level to do likewise. Consolidation, however, is not a code word for cutbacks. Adequate funding must be assured.

Finally, I believe that the library-using public should have more input into the decisions concerning the role of their local libraries. A nationwide series of library conferences culminating in a White House Conference is one method of implementing this process.

Libraries are a national resource, and all of the nation must share in their upkeep. By the same token all of the nation must have access to the information contained in our many and diverse libraries. The strength of our system of government is the collective wisdom of our people. Our libraries are one crucial foundation of that wisdom.

APPENDIX D

Library Bill of Rights

Adopted June 18, 1948. Amended February 2, 1961, and June 27, 1967, by the ALA Council.

The Council of the American Library Association reaffirms its belief in the following basic policies which should govern the services of all libraries.

1. As a responsibility of library service, books and other library materials selected should be chosen for values of interest, information and enlightenment of all the people of the community. In no case should library materials be excluded because of the race or nationality or the social, political, or religious views of the authors.

2. Libraries should provide books and other materials presenting all points of view concerning the problems and issues of our times; no library materials should be proscribed or removed from libraries because of partisan or doctrinal disapproval.

3. Censorship should be challenged by libraries in the maintenance

of their responsibility to provide public information and enlightenment.

4. Libraries should cooperate with all persons and groups concerned with resisting abridgment of free expression and free access to ideas.

5. The rights of an individual to the use of a library should not be denied or abridged because of his age, race, religion, national origins or social or political views.

6. As an institution of education for democratic living, the library should welcome the use of its meeting rooms for socially useful and cultural activities and discussion of current public questions. Such meeting places should be available on equal terms to all groups in the community regardless of the beliefs and affiliations of their members, provided that the meetings be open to the public.

APPENDIX E

The Freedom to Read

This set of propositions is contained in a statement originally issued in May 1953 by the Westchester Conference of the American Library Association and the American Book Publishers Council, now the Association of American Publishers. Adopted June 25, 1953. Revised January 28, 1972, by the ALA Council.

1. It is in the public interest for publishers and librarians to make available the widest diversity of views and expressions, including those which are unorthodox or unpopular with the majority.
2. Publishers, librarians, and booksellers do not need to endorse every idea or presentation contained in the books they make available. It would conflict with the public interest for them to establish their own political, moral, or aesthetic views as a standard for determining what books should be published or circulated.
3. It is contrary to the public interest for publishers or librarians to determine the acceptability of a book on the basis of the personal history or political affiliations of the author.
4. There is no place in our society for efforts to coerce the taste of

others, to confine adults to the reading matter deemed suitable for adolescents, or to inhibit the efforts of writers to achieve artistic expression.

5. It is not in the public interest to force a reader to accept with any book the prejudgment of a label characterizing the book or author as subversive or dangerous.

6. It is the responsibility of publishers and librarians, as guardians of the people's freedom to read, to contest encroachments upon that freedom by individuals or groups seeking to impose their own standards or tastes upon the community at large.

7. It is the responsibility of publishers and librarians to give full meaning to the freedom to read by providing books that enrich the quality and diversity of thought and expression. By the exercise of this affirmative responsibility, bookmen can demonstrate that the answer to a bad book is a good one, the answer to a bad idea is a good one.

The freedom to read is of little consequence when expended on the trivial; it is frustrated when the reader cannot obtain matter fit for his purpose. What is needed is not only the absence of restraint, but the positive provision of opportunity for the people to read the best that has been thought and said. Books are the major channel by which the intellectual inheritance is handed down, and the principal means of its testing and growth. The defense of their freedom and integrity, and the enlargement of their service to society, requires of all bookmen the utmost of their faculties, and deserves of all citizens the fullest of their support.

We state these propositions neither lightly nor as easy generalizations. We here stake out a lofty claim for the value of books. We do so because we believe that they are good, possessed of enormous variety and usefulness, worthy of cherishing and keeping free. We realize that the application of these propositions may mean the dissemination of ideas and manners of expression that are repugnant to many persons. We do not state these propositions in the comfortable belief that what people read is unimportant. We believe rather that what people read is deeply important; that ideas can be dangerous; but that the suppression of ideas is fatal to a democratic society. Freedom itself is a dangerous way of life, but it is ours.

APPENDIX F

The Right to Know

The following are representative statements by modern-day journalists on the role of the public library as a basic source of information for the news media.

The Christian Science Monitor has its own research library and clipping files, but, nevertheless, we do make considerable use of the Boston Public Library. Some of this comes under the heading of historic research where we need reference books that our library simply does not have the capacity to keep on hand. Another major category is contemporary information from specialized magazines, monographs, and papers. Quite often our Boston and New England reporters make use of BPL facilities in digging out background on a story or checking details from another source.

We feel the existence of such a storehouse of information is vital to our own role of giving the public as accurate news and analysis as possible.

Earl W. Foell, managing editor
The Christian Science Monitor

For detailed information on any given subject—trends in the motor industry, the genesis of a volcano—the library is irreplaceable as a news source.

Tom Dunning, city editor
The Evansville Courier

While it is true that most of the questions asked us by the reporting staff can be answered from previous editions of the paper and/or our own ready reference collection, it is equally true that we could not provide thorough and adequate research service without the public library. Use of the public library is such that a "library run" is scheduled almost daily.

Michele Ann Kapecky, librarian
Detroit Free Press

As do most newspapers, we have a large library of our own, not only of clippings but also of reference works, magazines, and the like. However, for reference purposes and for verification of facts—particularly in writing features—the Public Library is an essential asset to newspapers large or small. This would be particularly true in preparation of material for editorial pages.

W. W. Baker, president
The Kansas City Star

It is difficult for me to list in detail the countless times and ways in which we call on the public libraries here for help. Sometimes it may be only a matter of a quick phone call to determine a specific fact. On other occasions, a writer preparing a complicated article may spend hours in research at the library. The subject matter can range from energy policy to nineteenth-century vice presidents, from the inventor of the ice cream cone to the sociological history of Kenya. Our staff members seek from the public libraries anything that cannot be supplied by our own library or standard reference books.

Public libraries are an essential source for newspapers and, through them, for their readers.

Evarts A. Graham, managing editor
St. Louis Post-Dispatch

The news staff of the *N&O* makes frequent use of the Wake County library system to supplement its own reference sources. We have found particularly useful the public library's files of periodicals and special interest volumes. Reporters often have occasion to use these for background before going out on interview stories. The library's collection of business reference works also has been helpful.

Obviously, public libraries are of vital importance to journalists, authors, and the public. At a time when man's knowledge is growing in quantum leaps, the nation's libraries are an essential guide.

Guy Munger, city editor
The News and Observer [Raleigh, N.C.]

The Hamilton County Public Library is a civic asset, one which helps us day after day to put out a better newspaper.

Luke Feck, executive editor
The Cincinnati Enquirer

Suffice it to say that our entire staff are frequent users of library services, to supplement our own newspaper library. As a matter of fact, I will be paying a visit to the public library this afternoon to do some research on cross-over voting in primary elections!

Walter Friedenberg, editor
The Cincinnati Post

The *Dispatch* library uses the Public Library of Columbus & Franklin County between ten and fifteen times a week. Occasionally we will use other public libraries throughout the state of Ohio. The ready availability of this reference service gives us access to great information resources without the expense of buying large numbers of reference books and services. We use the library: To obtain biographical information, government documents, business information, and marketing information. We also use the research tools available at the library such as indexes, periodical collections, and the *New York Times* Information Bank.

James Hunter, librarian
The Columbus Dispatch

I make extensive use of both the voluminous Pennsylvania State Library and the lesser but adequate Harrisburg Public Library. Both are within four blocks of my newspaper office, and for me serve as an annex to the morgue of my paper.

No public libraries? That is as inconceivable to me as if there weren't a public water supply.

Paul B. Beers, associate editor
The Patriot [Harrisburg, Pa.]

The *Bulletin* library is nearly self-sufficient, but we do have occasion to use Philadelphia's famed Free Library system. When we do the results are enormously gratifying.

B. Dale Davis, executive editor
The Evening and Sunday Bulletin [Philadelphia]

Public libraries are, of course, valuable not only to journalists but to authors and all other citizens involved in the research for information.

Frank N. Hawkins, editor
Pittsburgh Post-Gazette

We borrow books, magazines, periodicals, informational texts and other materials from the Seattle Public Library several times a week. We also telephone the public library for information required by our writers, editors, reporters, ad persons, and others.

We need special information ranging from art to zoology. Example: We might need an obscure quote—or it seems obscure—after searching through over fifty books, not including the Bible, in our library. We phone the public library and "they" come up with the quote from the 52nd book we do not have!

Jack Doughty, executive editor
Seattle Post-Intelligencer

We have our own library staffed by four persons. However, the Tacoma Public Library is of vital importance to this newspaper. Through a coordination program established with the Northwest Room, the library provides us with a variety of information. On a weekly basis, it provides pictures and background material on artists appearing in our arts and entertainment edition, and historical information in our Sunday paper, for our women's section, and in the Time Machine, which recounts interesting items of our historical past.

Because of our program with the library, we can promise reporters books and magazines they request to be delivered in one day.

Donald A. Pugnetti, editor
The News Tribune [Tacoma, Wash.]

The *Wisconsin State Journal* has only a basic collection of reference books for staff use. It is growing but far from what is needed in the way of research, whether technical data or background, so we turn frequently to the public library.

The Madison Public Library provides prompt answers to simple reference questions, while cooperating at all times when we need background information for special stories or series. Occasionally, we have used their picture resources to illustrate a story. We use their periodical collection regularly.

Robert H. Spiegel, editor
Wisconsin State Journal

The public library is an invaluable supplemental aid to our own *Journal* library simply because its resources of books, periodicals, and publications are so much greater.

Writers for the City Room, as well as special section people ask for help to develop stories on subjects ranging from the obvious to the obscure. I do more detailed investigation for the special feature people who simply announce they want to do a story on such and such a subject. Would I get the material? Often the research work involved can't be satisfied in our own library. It is a matter of checking the public library's special indices and obtaining enough pertinent information.

T. B. Arnold, librarian
The Milwaukee Journal

Modern, well-supplied, easily accessible libraries are as essential to the public's continuing right to learn as are daily newspapers, radio, and television.

Charles L. Bennett, executive editor
Daily Oklahoman

Research, of course, is a direct benefit of adequately stocked libraries. And the public's right to know is meaningless without access to information sources and periodicals, whether they can afford to buy them on their own or not.

Libraries provide the perfect information retrieval system. As Isaac Asimov once observed: books impart their knowledge privately, personally, at your own convenience, and without any other equipment than your own eyes. And it uses up no extra energy.

Bern Sharfman, editorial page editor
Harrisburg [Pa.] *Patriot*

It is impossible to put too much importance on the role of public libraries in a democratic society. They offer everyone, from the richest to the poorest, equal access to information, the true source of power and influence.

In addition, libraries encourage literacy, a quality which needs to be more effectively promoted if newspapers and books are to continue as useful repositories for facts which readers can consider and form their own opinions.

Robert T. Seymour, executive editor
Harrisburg [Pa.] *Patriot*

I grew up in a library and I continue to visit one weekly. I can't imagine a world without them. That is why the big-city trend to reduce services, with libraries and museums regarded as fringe services that can be cut back first, is alarming. How sad it is that we have millions for elaborate sports stadiums but close the libraries on weekends. This sports fan feels that somewhere along the line we have lost our sense of priority.

B. Dale Davis
Philadelphia Bulletin

As a journalist and author, I am acutely aware of the importance of our nation's public libraries as a basic information resource. I have no hesitation in saying that our public libraries are absolutely essential to that unique American institution—the First Amendment.

The starting place for any journalist on a "big story" is his public library. Cut off this source and you impair the freedom of the press. Unfortunately, that is exactly what is going on today in our country. Public libraries are closing their doors or reducing hours in community after community. Authors—particularly those who are holding down full-time jobs—find libraries are no longer open at night when they want to do research. America's literary output is bound to suffer in the long run if this situation is not corrected at once.

The obvious answer lies in dependable long-range federal funding for public libraries, in partnership with state and local government.

Theodore H. White

APPENDIX G

For Further Information . . .

Associations and Agencies

American Library Association (ALA)
50 East Huron Street
Chicago, Illinois 60611

The chief spokesman for libraries in North America, ALA is the largest (35,000 members), the oldest (founded 1876), and most influential nongovernmental library organization in the world. Membership is open to librarians, libraries, trustees, friends of libraries, and others interested in the responsibilities of libraries in the educational, social, and cultural needs of society. Individual memberships are $35 a year.

Public Library Association (PLA)
50 East Huron Street
Chicago, Illinois 60611

A division of the American Library Association, the PLA's mission is to advance the development, effectiveness, and financial support of public library service to the American people; to speak for the library profession at the national level on matters pertaining to public libraries; and to enrich the professional competence and opportunities of public librarians. PLA is organized into sections and committees to offer, for example, help to small and medium-sized libraries in solving problems unique to them, to help libraries with the information they need to get information and referral services going, to design life-long learning programs for independent learners including illiterates, to preserve and promote ethnic and cultural heritages, and so on. The association keeps its members abreast of the latest research, issues, and trends through its quarterly newsletter, *Public Libraries*. Membership is open to members of the American Library Association at $15 a year for an individual membership.

National Commission on Libraries and Information Science
1717 K Street, N.W.
Suite 601
Washington, D.C. 20036

Created in 1970 as a permanent, independent agency within the executive branch of the federal government. The agency is charged with the task of developing and recommending plans for the provision of library and information services and for the coordination of activities at the federal, state, and local levels necessary to meet the library and information needs of the nation more effectively. The commission is responsible for planning and conducting the 1979 White House Conference on Library and Information Services.

Office of Libraries and Learning Resources
Office of Education
U.S. Department of Health, Education, and Welfare
Washington, D.C. 20202

Established by Congress in 1974 to administer the Library Services and Construction Act (LSCA) and other federally funded programs in the Office of Education related to assistance for libraries, information centers, and educational technology. The Library Services and Construction Act is the primary source for federal matching grant funds to strengthen public library service. For each of the fiscal years 1977 and 1978, appropriations amounted to $56,900,000. For 1979: $62,500,000. LSCA Title I (Public Library Services) provides grants to states to promote development of services in areas without service or with inadequate service, to strengthen services to such specialized groups as disadvantaged, handicapped, institutionalized; to strengthen state agency administration of LSCA and to strengthen metropolitan libraries to serve as national and regional resource centers. Under Titles II and III funds are appropriated for building construction and interlibrary cooperation.

Council on Library Resources
One Dupont Circle
Washington, D.C. 20036

Established by the Ford Foundation in 1956, the Council is the only major foundation devoted specifically to supporting library projects. It has supported significant efforts in bibliographic access, preservation, micrographics, library technology, library management, automation, networks, standards, services to users, resource development, and professional development for librarians.

National Citizens Emergency Committee to Save Our Public Libraries
Box 366
Bowling Green Station
New York, New York 10004

The National Citizens Emergency Committee to Save Our Public Libraries was organized in the spring of 1976 at a time when libraries in San Francisco, Detroit, Cleveland, Philadelphia, New York—and in scores of large and small communities in between—were feeling the impact of new budget cuts while runaway inflation had already strained their resources. The basic mission of the committee is to represent the concerns of members of the general public who are library users. The committee has focused its main attention on the need for improving library services through a national library program, and for providing a meaningful level of operating funds through a federal-state-local partnership. The committee publishes a Volunteer's Kit and periodic Newsletter for citizens who enlist as members of local Citizens

Committees for Public Libraries. Interested library users who would like to volunteer can obtain further information from the above address.

Urban Libraries Council
1101 North Third Street
Las Cruces, New Mexico 88001

An organization of over a hundred member libraries, the Council represents the interests of public libraries in cities with populations over 100,000. It has been an effective advocate for more federal funding for hard-pressed city libraries under the Library Services and Construction Act. ULC publishes an occasional newspaper for distribution by member libraries, entitled *Library News*.

Directories and Encyclopedias

The ALA Yearbook—an authoritative and readable source of information about activities, events, and organizations that reflect the diverse interests of the American Library Association.

Bowker Annual of Library and Book Trade Information—commonly known as the *Bowker Annual,* this is an excellent compilation of current statistics, directory information, and state of the art reports.

Encyclopedia of Library and Information Science—since 1968 twenty-two volumes have appeared. There are more to come. The encyclopedia carries in-depth articles covering the widest possible range of subjects in the field including articles about libraries in other countries.

Periodicals

American Libraries—eleven readable issues a year, the magazine of the American Library Association.

Library Journal—semimonthly, carries extensive coverage of library news and opinion. The single most useful magazine for keeping up with developments in the field.

Library Trends—quarterly, scholarly evaluations of current thought and practice, the leader in a large field.

Library Trustee Newsletter—a new bimonthly publication treats library concerns from the need-to-know viewpoint of the local policy-level decision maker. Available at $24.95 a year, P.O. Box 110, Glen Ridge, New Jersey 07028.

Public Library Quarterly—a new scholarly journal (and the only one concerned solely with public library issues), edited by the director of the Graduate School of Library and Information Science at the University of Tennessee. The first issue is due spring 1979.

School Library Journal—monthly, for those who want to keep up with public and school library services for children and young adults.

Wilson Library Journal—monthly, focuses each issue on a particular trend or problem but also includes many columns of regular library news.

Current Reading

Libraries for Today and Tomorrow by Virginia H. Mathews. Garden City, New York: Doubleday, 1976. A lively look at school and public libraries—how do we pay for them, who uses them, who staffs them, what are their services.

Library Programs Worth Knowing About prepared by Ann Erteschik, The State and Public Library Services Branch, Office of Libraries and Learning Resources. Washington, D.C., 1977. A descriptive, annotated catalogue of sixty-two outstanding projects originally funded under the Library Services and Construction Act. Available at the Office of Libraries and Learning Resources, 7th and D Streets, S.W., Room 3124, Washington, D.C. 20202.

The Library Connection compiled by the Public Library Association, a division of the American Library Association. Chicago: American Library Association, 1977. Essays written in praise of public libraries by Jacob Javits, Nat Hentoff, Sol Urick, Norman Cousins, George Plimpton, and others.

The Public Library: Its Circumstances and Prospects published in *Library Quarterly,* October 1978. Proceedings of a conference at the Graduate Library School of the University of Chicago in April 1978.

History of Libraries in the Western World by Elmer D. Johnson and Michael H. Harris. Metuchen, New Jersey: Scarecrow Press, 1976. An extremely readable history of libraries from earliest times to the present. Fascinating background information for anyone involved in library work.

OF SPECIAL INTEREST TO FRIENDS OF THE LIBRARY

Two action-oriented manuals designed to take interested citizens step-by-step through the activities needed to develop a group of library supporters, from creating the organization to developing communications to assisting with membership drives and building campaigns:

Find Out Who Your Friends Are, available at $5 from: Patricia A. Boyle, Friends of the Free Library of Philadelphia, Logan Square, Philadelphia, Pennsylvania 19103.

The California Extension Kit, a newly revised edition of this standby is available for $5 from Friends of California Libraries, P.O. Box 455, Sierra Madre, California 91024.

The following publications are available from the Library Administration and Management Association, a division of the American Library Association, 50 East Huron Street, Chicago, Illinois 60611:

A Directory of Friends of Libraries Groups in the United States—gives basic information about more than 2,000 groups with the purpose of providing an awareness of the existence of other friends groups and thereby to make possible exchanges of information between groups.

Friends of the Library National Notebook—a four-page quarterly newsletter with articles on happenings nationally in the world of Friends, news of local activities and programs that may suggest useful ideas for other Friends groups, ALA news of interest to Friends. $4 a year.

Prepare! The Library Public Relations Recipe Book, compiled and edited by Irene Moran. How-to information on doing news releases, newsletters, graphics, tips on speaking, writing annual reports, getting on the air, and so on. Aimed primarily at librarians, but of interest to Friends as well. $4 a copy.